EDUCATION FOR CARE

Communication in Nursing Care

Edited by

WILL BRIDGE BSc PhD
Senior Research Officer
Joint Board of Clinical Nursing Studies
London
and
JILL MACLEOD CLARK BSc SRN
Department of Nursing Studies Chelsea College,
University of London

with 8 contributors

Foreword by

DAME PHYLLIS FRIEND DBE
Chief Nursing Officer
Department of Health and Social Security
London

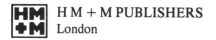

H M + M PUBLISHERS
London

© HM + M Publishers Ltd 1981

HM+M HM + M PUBLISHERS LTD ARE A DIVISION OF
HEYDEN & SON LTD

England — Spectrum House, Hillview Gardens, London NW4 2JQ
Germany — Devesburgstrasse 6, 4440 Rheine
U.S.A. — 247 South 41st Street, Philadelphia, PA 19104

ISBN 0 85602 083 4

Printed in Great Britain by Mackays of Chatham Ltd, Lordswood,
Chatham, Kent

CONTRIBUTORS

PAT ASHWORTH MSc SRN SCM FRCN
World Health Organisation Programme Manager
University of Manchester

JENIFER WILSON BARNETT BA MSc PhD SRN Dip. in Nursing (Lond)
Lecturer in Nursing Studies
Chelsea College, University of London

SENGA BOND BA MSc PhD RGN CMBPt1
Nursing Research Liaison Officer, Northern Regional Health
Authority; Senior Lecturer, Newcastle-upon-Tyne Polytechnic

WILL BRIDGE BSc PhD
Senior Research Officer
Joint Board of Clinical Nursing Studies, London

JILL MACLEOD CLARK BSc SRN
Department of Nursing Studies Chelsea College,
University of London

PAULINE FIELDING BSc SRN
Nursing Research Fellow, Department of Psychology
University of Southampton

MAGGIE HACKING SRN
Formerly Sister, Home Care Team
St. Christopher's Hospice, London

JUNE JOLLY SRN RSCN SocStudCert
Member, Advisory Panel for Children in Hospital, Consumers'
Association; formerly Paediatric Liaison Nursing Officer
Greenwich & Bexley Area Health Authority

JEAN McINTOSH BSc PhD SRN CMBPt1
Formerly Research Fellow, Department of General Practice
University of Aberdeen

ISABEL SPEIGHT RMN SRN HVCert RNT
Professional Officer
Joint Board of Clinical Nursing Studies, London

Contents

Foreword

Everyone in the nursing profession pays lip-service to the importance of communication. However, the fact that we are forced to give so much time and thought to the subject bears testimony both to its complexity and to the fact that there is still so much to be learned about it. Good communication in health care is not easy to achieve – it has to be worked at, and one way of learning to communicate more effectively is to explore the subject in books such as this one. I am sure that all nurses and other readers will find in this book much that they can use to improve standards of care, and for this reason I am pleased to contribute this foreword.

The dominant theme of the book is that communication is not an optional extra in nursing care, but a central feature of the role of the nurse. Hospital wards where communication is effective are not simply more pleasant places to be in; this book shows that they are also places in which patients recover more quickly, and suffer less pain and anxiety. Three other particularly important and practical aspects emerge. The first is that communication can be, and indeed must be, matched to patients' own needs. The second is that, despite many nurses' belief to the contrary, communication in nursing *can* be taught and learned effectively. The third point is that the contributors to this book do not assume that communication by nurses takes place in a vacuum. They discuss the communication roles of others and give good examples, including those of doctors in the case of patients with cancer, and relatives where children or the elderly are involved. All the chapters have been carefully integrated to ensure that the book reads as a whole, and is not just a collection of essays about aspects of the subject – this enhances its value.

Because communication is so central to nursing care, I welcome this book not only as a textbook about a part of nursing practice called 'communication', but as a book about nursing itself. As such it is a valuable addition to the literature.

PHYLLIS FRIEND
London 1981

Preface

This book is about communication between nurses and patients. In it we show that communicating with patients and relatives is fundamental to every aspect of nursing care, and illustrate the wide variety of issues and problems which are subsumed under the deceptively simple label of 'communication'. The variety of the contributed chapters also shows that nurses must develop a range of insights and skills in order to communicate effectively with patients and relatives. These include practical skills which will help to overcome problems such as communicating with deaf or semi-conscious patients. However, certain more philosophical questions related to the information which should be given to a dying patient, or the degree to which nurses should become 'involved' when caring for patients, are also examined.

This book represents the first attempt in the UK to set down in one place a collection of some of the many factors and issues involved when nurses communicate with patients. We felt that, given current levels of knowledge and understanding, this was not a task for one or two people to undertake alone. In consequence, the book is a co-operative effort, with individual authors bringing to it their own particular specialised knowledge, insight and experience.

The contributors have pursued widely different careers, although all are experienced nurses. As a result, the different chapters explore ways in which a range of fields of study, including several outside nursing, such as psychology, sociology and counselling, can illuminate aspects of nurse-patient communication.

The description and analysis of communication in nursing presented throughout the book draws upon two key sources – research evidence, and the personal experience of our contributors. The book also contains many practical suggestions for changes which can improve nurse-patient communication.

Research data presented throughout the book emphasises that such improvements are of vital importance. For example, a number of studies of the effects of improved communication upon patients' recovery periods and levels of stress are quoted in this book. These all serve to underline a point which recurs throughout that close communication with patients is not merely a pleasant 'optional extra' in nursing; it is critical for the physical and physiological wellbeing of patients, and the development of nursing as a caring profession.

The picture of the current *status quo* in nurse-patient communication presented by some of the research studies reported in this book is, in parts, both disturbing and unsatisfactory. Different contributors provide different explanations for this, but all conclude that factors such as the lack of education and training, and an unfavourable climate in the wards can inhibit nurse-patient communication. These issues are discussed in detail in the final chapter of the book.

When we first planned this book we were convinced that the ability to communicate effectively with patients was very near to the heart of nursing. Our contributors have convinced us even further of this, since each chapter seems to capture the real essence of caring for patients as people rather than as cases, bed-numbers or problems.

We are grateful to our colleagues who, like us, have recognised the importance of communication in patient care, and greatly encouraged us as the book took shape. The Communication Study Group at the Joint Board of Clinical Nursing Studies provided an important stimulus for this work and we would like to acknowledge their support, and that of our friends at Chelsea College, London. We are grateful also to Mary Hansford who so patiently helped with the typing of the manuscript. Finally, the book would never have seen the light of day without one vital group of people: our contributors. We hope they are still our friends!

WILL BRIDGE
JILL MACLEOD CLARK
London 1981

Chapter 1

Nursing and Communication

Jill Macleod Clark   Will Bridge

Communication between nurses* and patients, and the 'nurse-patient relationship' are two of the most complex and least understood aspects of nursing. This book attempts to unravel some of this complexity, and provoke readers into thinking about many important issues related to nurse-patient communication. These issues are as diverse as how nurses can deal with patients who are anxious or in pain, how to anticipate and cope with feelings of over-involvement with patients, and how to prepare patients for different aspects of their treatment.

Patients need communication

There is already a good deal of evidence to show that patients themselves view communication as an issue which is central to their care. For example, a number of research surveys carried out over the past two decades have demonstrated that patients tend to be more critical about poor communication between staff and patients than about any other aspect of their hospital experience (Cartwright 1964; Raphael 1969; Skeet 1970). More recent research (Reynolds 1978) has shown that over half of the patients interviewed on a surgical ward were dissatisfied with the amount of information they received. Moreover, patients are *right* to be concerned about the effectiveness of communication. It has been established that giving adequate information and explanation before operations or investigations can result in tangible benefits to patients in terms of

*For simplicity, we have adopted the convention of using the term 'nurse' in this book to include midwives and health visitors as well, and have tended to ascribe the feminine gender to the nurse, and the masculine gender to the patient.

1

reduced pain and discomfort, reduced anxiety and reduced stress (Wilson Barnett 1978; Hayward 1975; Boore 1978). Although these studies concentrated upon patient's reactions to specific investigations or surgical procedures, there is every reason to expect that patients will benefit from information and explanation in many other situations. Equally, it seems likely that other forms of communication, such as asking questions, allowing patients to express their feelings, or reassuring patients by means of touch will also result in improved patient care, and increased patient satisfaction and well-being.

The need for education

There is an apparent contradiction in nursing today which manifests itself as follows: while an increasing emphasis is placed in nursing education upon meeting the psychological and emotional needs of patients as well as their physical needs, this emphasis is rarely translated into active teaching programmes. The growing interest in applying the nursing process in planning patient care (Hunt & Marks-Maran 1980) requires nurses to take communication with patients more seriously than ever before. Indeed, the principle of individualised patient care planning requires the nurse to establish a close relationship with her patient. Moreover, if the processes of taking admission histories and planning and evaluating care are undertaken properly they will inevitably bring nurses and patients into closer contact with each other.

However, as a general rule, very little time is allocated during most nurse training programmes to the discussion of issues related to communicating with patients. In addition, it is rare for time to be set aside specifically for nurses to learn the skills of communication or to practise such skills in situations where they are helped and constructively criticised.

If nurses are to learn to communicate better with their patients it is essential that they should become more aware of the complexity of this process called 'communication'. Patients have a wide range of communication needs. These can be thought of as being on a kind of continuum (Fig. 1.1) which goes from the need for simple social interaction or contact at one end to the need for skilled counselling at the other.

- SOCIAL INTERACTION
- INFORMATION
- ADVICE
- REASSURANCE
- DISCUSSION OF DIAGNOSIS, TREATMENT AND PROGNOSIS
- DISCUSSION OF FEELINGS
- COUNSELLING

Fig. 1.1   Patients' communication needs

Figure 1.1 illustrates the diversity of possible communication needs of patients. The list is not definitive and there is considerable overlap between the different categories of need. Not every patient has a need for all these forms of communication, although at a guess nearly every patient will benefit from some social contact with nurses and most probably require information of some kind. Although there is no strict order attached to the needs listed, there are certain important relationships within the continuum. For example, while social interaction and giving information are activities which can occur at a 'superficial' level, it is impossible to communicate in terms of 'discussion of feelings' or 'counselling' without the existence of a deeper or more established nurse-patient relationship. Thus, the lower end of the continuum reflects communication needs which may require greater skill, experience and involvement on the part of the nurse. This increased involvement may in turn result in emotional conflicts which can be threatening for the nurse.

In addition to recognising the enormous range and diversity of patients' possible communication needs, it is also necessary for all nurses to be aware of the many factors which can affect communication with patients. These factors arise from the environment in which nurses and patients try to communicate, an environment which can be stressful, noisy or disturbing. However, communication is also affected by the fact that nurses and patients are all individuals — with different strengths and weaknesses and different needs, attitudes and perceptions.

Communication is a notoriously difficult subject to teach, and there is little tangible guidance available at the moment for nurses and their teachers. One problem is the fact that the term 'communication' means many different things to many different people. This implies that the number of topics which could be covered in a book on communication in nursing, even one concentrating upon nurse-patient communication alone is enormous. Indeed, a great deal has been written elsewhere about nursing communication in the most general terms. Much of this general literature is characterised by the tendency simply to advocate or encourage nurses to somehow communicate 'better'. Far less has been written about particular aspects of nurse-patient communication in terms precise enough for the reader to learn exactly what factors might help them to become 'better' at it; or how they might 'improve the system'; or what 'better' communication might imply for the patient and the nurse.

An eclectic approach

The approach taken in compiling this book has involved gathering together chapters from eight contributors, each of whom has a specialist interest in communication in a certain area of nursing. In addition, each chapter takes a different approach to the description of nurse-patient communication so that, for example, some concentrate on the communication of facts and information, whereas in others the emphasis is upon the interpersonal and emotional aspects of communication between nurses and patients. This approach is intended to provide a thought-provoking basis which will help nurses to discuss, teach, and practise this vital aspect of nursing.

The first contributed chapter, Chapter 2, is on communicating with patients in general medical or surgical wards, and was contributed by Jenifer Wilson Barnett, who is an experienced nurse researcher. Accordingly, she describes a number of studies, including her own, which have demonstrated that improvements in communication can actually improve the patients' well-being and rate of recovery. Chapter 3 relies much more heavily upon the personal experience of its author, June Jolly, who contributes an extensive and international perspective on the little-researched subject of communication in paediatric nursing. A similar picture prevails in geriatric nursing, and Pauline Fielding's chapter looks at the implications of communicating with the elderly, who form a growing proportion of the patients being cared for in hospital.

The intensive care unit is unique in many respects, not least in the kinds of communication which are possible and necessary there. Pat Ashworth has much experience of working in intensive care units, and has undertaken research into communication in intensive care nursing. She concentrates in her chapter on communicating with critically-ill patients who may be unconscious, semiconscious, or sensorily deprived as a result of their illness or treatment.

Chapter 6 is about communication in psychiatric nursing, and builds upon the fact that at least some of the nurses working in this field have long recognised that their role is mainly concerned with forming relationships with patients. Isabel Speight describes an area of knowledge that psychiatric nurses are becoming increasingly aware of, namely the verbal and non-verbal tactics which nurses can use to encourage patients to talk about their problems, and to explore with patients different ways of coping with their problems.

The two chapters which follow are on communication in community nursing, and communicating with cancer patients. They both take a rather different view of nurse-patient communication from that of preceding chapters – one that is basically sociological or social-psychological in nature. In the cancer nursing chapter, Senga Bond refers to cancer as a widely-feared disease. She also looks at the strategies which both nurses and patients develop in order to 'cope' with illness, pain and distress, and she describes the effects that these strategies can have when nurses and patients are attempting to communicate with one another. The growing priority given to nursing care in the community is reflected in Jean McIntosh's chapter, much of which is based upon her own research studies which looked at the 'roles' adopted by nurses as they communicate with their patients from two distinct standpoints; that of the invited 'guest' in the house, and that of the 'professional nurse'.

In the final chapter on communicating with dying patients and their relatives, Maggie Hacking examines how changes in attitudes towards disease, dying and death can profoundly effect the nurse's relationship with her patients. This chapter is based upon the author's extensive personal experience in this area of nursing, and as such it is a realistic and human account of the difficulties and rewards of communicating with the dying.

Although each chapter of the book tackles a different area of nursing, the chapters have a great deal in common. Firstly, their approach to the problem of communication concentrates consistently upon communication between nurses and patients. While all the authors recognise the importance of communication between, say doctors and patients, and between nurses and doctors, these relationships are not the primary concern of this book. A further theme which runs throughout the book is that each chapter is given a 'research basis' wherever possible and is also written using the author's personal experience of nursing practice, education or research. The authors of certain chapters have carried out research related to nurse-patient communication in their own particular field, and they describe their findings and draw on other relevant research. Where the authors have not themselves carried out research, they review the research findings available which relate to their area of interest. The use of research findings is very important in a subject as complex as nurse-patient communication, since this is a subject which has long been hidden under generalisations, platitudes and clichés.

An attempt has been made in each chapter to present a range of different ideas and perspectives. Some of these are deliberately provocative and are included in this book with the specific purpose of raising as many issues as possible. Again, while most chapters contain practical suggestions for improving communication, there is only a limited amount of prescriptive advice. This is a reflection of our limited knowledge of the art and science of communication. Indeed, many questions remain to be answered about the most effective, appropriate and desirable methods of communicating with patients.

Between them, the contributors have covered a large amount of material and discussed communication in relation to the needs of many different groups of patients. However, we do not claim to have achieved anything like definitive or comprehensive coverage in this book. Many of the issues discussed are relevant to all aspects of nursing care, but others are more specialised, and some issues require much deeper analysis than has been possible in a book of this size. There are also important nursing specialties which have not been covered, including obstetrics, gynaecology, family planning, ENT, health visiting, mental handicap, the out-patient department and accident and emergency nursing. It will take another book to cover the communication needs of patients in these groups, and the further range of issues and problems which emerge in these settings.

Nurses with specialised knowledge and skills have much to offer their colleagues working in other fields of patient care. The chapters which follow show that this is particularly true in understanding nurse-patient communication. We hope that readers will recognise the relevance of those chapters which relate to fields of nursing other than their own. For example, the techniques of encouraging patients to talk and of attentive listening described in the psychiatric nursing chapter should be learnt by all members of the profession. Likewise, the issues raised when communicating with children, the elderly, and the dying are ones which must be faced at some time by almost every nurse.

We have provided very short editorial commentaries at the beginning of each chapter. These are intended to guide readers through the book by giving an outline of each contributor's background and a brief description of the perspectives taken in each chapter. In the Postscript we have summarised the main issues which emerge throughout the book, and draw out some vital implications for improvements and changes in nursing practice, education and research.

References

Boore J. (1978) *A Prescription for Recovery.* London: RCN

Cartwright A (1964) *Human Relations and Hospital Care.* London: Routledge & Kegan Paul

Hayward J. (1975) *Information, a Prescription Against Pain.* London: RCN

Hunt J. & Marks-Maran D. (1980) *Nursing Care Plans: The Nursing Process at Work.* Aylesbury: H M + M Publishers

Raphael W. (1969) *Patients and their Hospitals.* King Edward's Hospital Fund for London

Reynolds M. (1978) No news is bad news: patients' views about communication in hospital. *British Medical Journal,* **1,** 1673–1676

Skeet M. (1970) *Home from Hospital.* Dan Mason Nursing Research Committee

Wilson-Barnett J. (1978) Patients' emotional response to barium X-rays. *Journal of Advanced Nursing,* **3,** 37–46

Chapter 2: Communicating with Patients in General Wards

In this chapter the topic of communication is examined in the context of the needs of patients who are admitted to general surgical or general medical wards. Most nurses would accept the fact that it is important to communicate effectively with patients. However, the direct relationship between the quality of information, explanation or support given by the nurse, and a patient's well-being is often less well understood. Therefore, the author has taken the deliberate step of describing, wherever possible, the research evidence *for the issues discussed.*

The majority of adults have at least one experience of hospitalisation during their lives, and a large proportion of them become patients on general wards. It is well recognised that an individual who is facing either hospital admission, an operation, or a routine investigation will suffer from some degree of anxiety. Research has demonstrated that explanation, support and appropriate information can significantly reduce such anxiety. Throughout this chapter a case is made for increasing the nurse's role and responsibility for all aspects of communication with patients.

The very nature of general wards means that a wide variety of patients are admitted to them and a vast range of nursing, medical and technical activities take place in such wards. Readers will recognise, therefore, that many of the ideas and principles expressed in this chapter are relevant to other fields of nursing. It seems likely that many of the patients' needs for information and explanation are universal, and the suggestions made for improving nurses' skills in these particular areas are valid in almost any other setting. The need for specific education in communication skills during nurse training is also highlighted in this chapter, and this emerges as an important and recurrent theme in every chapter in the book.

The author of this chapter, Jenifer Wilson Barnett, has had a varied nursing and academic career. She trained at St George's Hospital, London, and worked as a ward sister on a medical ward. She obtained a BA(Social Science) degree from Leicester University and took a two-year Master's degree course at Edinburgh University. She was awarded a PhD for her subsequent research in which she investigated patients' emotional reactions to hospitalisation, and in particular to barium X-ray examination. Her current research interests include an evaluation of the effect of counselling for hysterectomy patients prior to discharge from hospital, upon their subsequent recovery at home, and a follow-up study of patients' postoperative recovery after coronary artery bypass surgery.

Chapter 2

Communicating with Patients in General Wards

Jenifer Wilson Barnett

Introduction

This chapter looks at the whole field of nurse-patient communication in general medical and general surgical wards. Many articles have been written about the importance of 'good' communication in nursing, although the majority are couched in the most general terms and simply advocate 'better communication'. Much less has been written which explores the topic in any systematic way, basing tangible recommendations on research findings. This chapter represents a deliberate attempt to avoid generalisation, so that whenever possible, the value of communicating effectively with patients is discussed in the context of relevant findings.

Communication and the interactions which take place between nurses and patients is central to all nursing care, but there is much evidence, reviewed in this chapter, which suggests that nurse-patient communication in general wards could be improved. Although patients usually lavish praise on the nurses, claiming that they are very friendly and kind, there are also frequent comments, such as 'I didn't like to bother them, they are so busy' or 'well, nobody told me', or 'I was afraid of what would happen as I didn't know what to expect'. Patients' anxiety, lack of information, and reluctance to ask questions are some of the most obvious signs that nursing communication is not all that it might be.

A wide variety of adult patients of all ages are diagnosed and treated in general wards. They will have varying degrees of experience of hospitals, many different medical conditions, and their age range spans something like 70 years. For this reason, the principles of effective communication with general ward patients will hold for patient care in many other settings. One study which described the work of nurses in general wards (Rhys-Hearn 1968) found that it is basic needs for physical care which determine how much attention patients receive, and that it is the most junior nurses who spend most time communicating and interacting with patients. These factors obviously influence communication. A study by Menzies (1960) described interviews with student nurses in which they reported great feelings of anxiety and inadequacy about their work with patients. As student nurses spend more time with patients than do other nurses, they are likely to establish closer relationships, and they may attempt to be supportive by being very open with their patients. Menzies found that in this situation they were unable to cope with their patients' worries and distress. Inadequate support and guidance for these nurses eventually led them to take evasive steps to avoid these sustained conversations. Menzies' research concluded that more training in how to cope when supporting patients is essential for students and for the welfare of their patients.

In contrast to students, trained staff frequently complain about the pressures of administrative and paper work. Hockey (1976) found that they wanted to spend more time in talking to and reassuring patients, but that other work was always more pressing. Obviously those aspects of the work which are considered most important come first and those which have a lower priority such as talking to patients are only undertaken 'when there is time'. Therefore, it may be that nurses' priorities should be adjusted, but before considering this, the needs of patients must be assessed. If this demonstrates that patients feel that communication is inadequate and deserves a higher priority, it is likely that the pattern of nurse-patient communication in general wards should be altered and improved.

Patients' needs for communication

In 1969, Raphael undertook a survey that confirmed earlier studies indicating that patients have a great appreciation of nurses' warmth and friendliness, and that this is considered to be of great importance in determining the ward atmosphere. Her patients were most appreciative of the opportunity to chat, especially to other patients and the nursing staff. My own studies of patients' emotional responses to events in general medical wards have also shown that this opportunity to talk is a major factor in patients' adjustment to life in hospital (Wilson-Barnett & Carrigy 1978).

On the other hand, the concern most frequently expressed by patients is about their lack of information. Cartwright (1964) found that two-thirds of a general ward sample of patients would have liked to have been told more about their condition and treatment. However, even with a systematic plan to keep patients fully informed, it has been shown that a substantial proportion will be dissatisfied (Hugh Jones *et al.* 1964). Although many people have been concerned about this problem of giving patients adequate information, the situation does not seem to have altered in recent years. In my own research (Wilson-Barnett 1977) it was also found that 40% of all comments on this subject from a sample of patients from general medical wards confirmed their desire for more information. Such findings raise fundamental questions about why patients do not ask for more information, and why the staff do not seem to invite questions from patients. We do not know the answer to these questions yet, but it may be due to nurses' lack of awareness that information actually helps patients, or because they may be unable or are not allowed to answer the patients' questions adequately.

My own experience as a nurse and a researcher leads me to believe that for some patients this lack of knowledge leads to acute anxiety in the 'face of the unknown'. Unfortunately, it is these most distressed patients who are likely to remain without information or support. In her research, Stockwell (1972) attempted to determine which patients were the most 'popular' on the general wards, and she related this to those receiving most nursing attention. By interviewing the nurses about which patients they most enjoyed nursing and by observing their work, she was able to associate their opinions with their activities. She found that the unpopular patients and those receiving less attention generally were those who had been in hospital for the longest period of time, those who had a history of psychiatric illness or who had complained or showed signs of distress during their stay. While nurses' dislikes can prejudice patient care in this way, another influence is clearly a feeling of inadequacy to help patients in need of psychological care. Once more, these research findings confirm the value to both nurses and their patients of systematic communication skills training for nurses.

Disapproval towards those who express their need for comfort may be more general than is often recognised. A study by Coser (1965) using observation methods in a ward, described how patients as well as staff discouraged complaints or open signs of distress, such as crying, from newly-admitted patients. Other patients refused to befriend newcomers until they learned to adopt a humorous approach to their illness and problems.

Further work on how staff communicate with patients in need of comfort also emphasises how much patients are discouraged from asking for help and how signs of distress do not attract a desirable response from nurses. Maguire's study (1978) in which patients with breast cancer were interviewed and observed showed how rarely staff sit down and talk to patients who are clearly in a state of stress. Nurses tended to ignore signs of distress or offered platitudes such as 'don't worry' or 'it will be all right' and administered sedatives, rather than listening to patients or allowing them to talk about their worries. Eliciting questions from patients can be helpful in that answers can encourage a realistic understanding of the patient's condition. Many of the patients in Maguire's study were found to be most fearful of the spread of cancer and imminent death. As a proportion of these patients had a favourable prognosis, it is reasonable to expect that an accurate account of their condition would help these women. Maguire points out that since the patients' need for knowledge does not necessarily involve elaborate details, most nurses should be quite able to answer the usual, straight-forward questions.

My own research demonstrated that it is by no means always patients who *show* or *express* their distress who require the most psychological care (Wilson-Barnett & Carrigy 1978). When patients were interviewed, we found that it was the quietest, least expressive patients who often reported most anxiety and depression throughout their stay in medical wards. However, these patients often received the least attention from nurses although they were most at risk and most in need of support. For example, those who had been admitted for diagnostic tests or who had early stages of cancer were most likely to be very worried about their condition and to experience feelings of guilt. This could relate either to a lack of obvious serious debility, or to their worry that if the doctors could not make a diagnosis they may be considered as hypochondriacal.

Moffic & Paykel (1975) found that the most depressed group of patients were those who were seriously ill and, therefore, in need of careful attention from staff. Kubler Ross (1969) also reached a similar finding in her sample of American patients from general wards who had a terminal illness. These patients who were most in need of a systematic plan for communication and support felt deserted by the doctors. Perhaps the doctors' sense of failure made their visits more stressful and, therefore, less frequent. The doctors delegated many decisions to the nurses but in spite of this added responsibility, nurses also tended to leave these patients alone, apart from ministering to their basic physical needs. Loneliness was the one thing that most of these patients feared, and this fear became real due to the staff's inability to cope with their own feelings in the presence of these patients.

There is no doubt that particular groups of patients in general wards (such as the very anxious, the undiagnosed, the severely ill or the unsociable) require really open communication with staff so that their needs can be recognised and satisfied. Nurses should be in a position not only to know who might benefit from improved communication, but also what sort of improvements can be made. The research quoted so far establishes the value and need for nurses to communicate effectively by planning to allow time for conversation and for one-to-one contact. The next part of this chapter explores the value and effect of specific ways of improving communication by increasing the amount of information given to patients.

The nurse's role in giving information to patients

Being ill in hospital inevitably causes anxiety and stress in most patients. It is possible to identify certain aspects of hospital life, or events in the patients' hospital experience, which are particularly stressful, and it is worth examining both these events, and the nurses' role in alleviating them. It has been firmly established that patients' stress can indeed be reduced by giving them adequate and appropriate information and explanations (Siminov 1970). Anxiety is an unpleasant emotion and much unnecessary energy can be expended when patients' fears are unrealistic. With experience, nurses should be able to recognise that there can be a huge gap between the knowledge about procedures and conditions that they themselves possess and the knowledge that their patients possess. It is clearly important to try to narrow this gap from the moment the patient is admitted.

Admission to hospital   Patients can find admission more stressful than anything else which occurs during their stay in hospital, especially if they have never been in hospital before (Wilson-Barnett & Carrigy 1978). The anxiety generated by admission can be reduced by providing clear information which will be useful to the patient. Elms & Leonard (1966) showed how an explanation of what would happen in hospital, the facilities and usual events, the names of staff and their jobs, the meal times and ward geography and an introduction to other patients, all helped to make the patient and his relatives more at ease. By imagining what they need to know, and making an effort to satisfy these needs, patients' initial experiences in hospital could be far less stressful.

Diagnostic tests   Some of the most anxiety-producing procedures taking place on medical wards are 'special tests' such as barium X-rays and lumbar punctures. For this reason it is essential that nurses should recognise the patients' anxiety and concentrate on reducing their stress. Johnson *et al.* (1973) studied the procedure of gastroscopy in order to assess what type of explanation helped patients to cope with this. Of their sample of 99 patients, one-third were given a taped message explaining how the procedure would be carried out and how it would feel. Details of sights, sounds and sensations were included, and photographs were shown to the patients to give them a full picture of what to expect. The second group was given a taped message with procedural details only, and the control group was given no information about the procedure. The results confirmed that the fullest explanation was most effective in reducing patients' anxiety and helped them to prepare and cope with the procedure. The researchers concluded that the nearer the patients' anticipation of an event was to reality, the lower the level of fear and the greater the opportunity for adjustment.

This conclusion is by no means a matter of common sense, for many professionals withhold the truth about patients' future experiences believing that such information would merely increase and prolong their anxiety. For example, many radiographers believe this in the case of patients scheduled for barium enema. However, my own research (Wilson-Barnett 1977) has demonstrated the reverse. In a study with 58 patients for barium meal and 70 for barium enema, a five-minute verbal explanation accompanied by a written sheet of this explanation was given to half the patients in both groups. Their anxiety was measured by a simple self-report scale, and anxiety scores were compared between the informed and uninformed groups both before and during screening. The explanation of both these tests resulted in reduced levels of reported anxiety – this was most effective for barium enema patients who experienced the more stressful procedure. An example of the explanation given to patients during the research study is shown in Figure 2.1 overleaf.

This kind of full explanation is not usually given to patients, perhaps because such investigations seem commonplace to staff. However, given that we know that they can be very distressing to unprepared patients, it is essential that nurses undertake responsibility for giving their patients adequate explanations. The way the explanation is given, the words used (and their emphasis) all influence how useful the information will be. By talking to patients who have already experienced such a test, nurses can learn their vocabulary. They will then be able to use relevant descriptions of how painful or uncomfortable any given procedure is, how long the discomfort lasts, and perhaps gain some hints on how to make it more tolerable. The growing number of these diagnostic tests makes it more important to talk to patients and learn about their reactions to them, especially as it may not always be possible for nurses to witness them in the laboratories or departments.

Surgical operations Surgical operations obviously cause much stress and worry. Carnevali (1966) found that patients fear pain and anaesthesia most, but she also found that nurses underestimate how much patients worry about these aspects of surgery. When nurses in this study were asked how they comforted their patients, they tended to rely only upon the giving of information. However, their patients emphasised the nurses' warmth and friendliness, apparently unaware of her efforts to impart information. Such findings reinforce the view that it is not only the type of information but the way in which it is communicated which is of greatest importance.

Hayward (1975) and Boore (1979) undertook studies which assessed the effects of giving information to pre-operative patients

EXPLANATION TO PATIENTS FOR A BARIUM ENEMA

The purpose of this procedure is to X-ray the bowels and back passage. By passing barium into the bowels through the back passage an outline of the lower bowel can be seen. If there is anything wrong with these parts it may show up on these X-rays.

In order for the bowel or intestines to show clearly, they must be completely empty of waste materials. So the day before you must eat food that has little waste materials in it, such as dry biscuits, plain bread, lean meat, clear fruit jelly and clear soup. All this food will be sent from the diet kitchen. Also to clear the tubes you should drink plenty of water, at least a glass full at 1 pm, 3 pm, 7 pm, and one before bed on the day before your X-ray. Also on the night before your X-ray, at about 8 pm, the ward nurse will give you a glass of specially prepared solution to drink. This will be followed at 10 pm by three tablets to be swallowed with a glass or more of water. All this preparation is to ensure the bowel is empty, but you can have a light breakfast on the morning of your X-ray.

On the morning of your X-ray the ward staff will give you a suppository, which is to be inserted into your back passage as high as possible. This procedure is slightly uncomfortable, but not painful. It is important for you to try to retain the suppository for about 15 minutes, if possible, before going to the toilet. Prior to your X-ray you will be given a gown by the ward staff and you may also wear your dressing gown and slippers when the porter comes to collect you and take you to the X-ray department. On arrival at the department you may be required to wait for a short time before being shown into the X-ray room. In this room where the main lights are turned off at the start of the procedure, there will be odd trolleys and pieces of X-ray equipment. The main X-ray camera, which takes films shown on a television and ordinary X-rays, is a solid box suspended from the ceiling. It moves up and down and along the length of the table. The X-ray table, where the patient lies, is metal and solid and feels rather hard, but is covered by a paper cloth and pad in case any barium is spilt. The camera is worked from behind a screen by the wall and by a foot pedal near the table by the doctor. The doctor stands beside the table and directs the procedure and takes the films, and the radiographer takes the permanent 'still' X-rays from behind the screen. She also changes the film plates in the camera. The staff all wear special aprons to protect them from too much X-ray.

When the doctor comes, he may ask you a few questions about your illness and look at your X-rays. With you lying on your front he will then insert a plastic enema tube into your back passage, which may be a little uncomfortable, but you will get used to it. This tube is closed off or opened to let in the barium, by the doctor. The doctor may also pump in a little air as this shows up more of the bowels for the X-rays. You may now be asked to change your position, from side to side, and on to your back, and periodically to hold your breath. The table may be tilted head down or feet down, and this makes a slight noise, as does the movement of the camera. In all, the procedure will take 30-40 minutes. When all the X-rays are taken you may have to wait for the doctor to see the last pictures. He may not be able to tell you straight away what he has found as he needs to study them very carefully.

Before you empty your bowels, the radiographer may want to take a few more shots with you on your side, leaning against a side support fixed to the table. She will then guide you to the nearest toilet. For these few last minutes you may feel rather blown-out and also eager to empty your bowel. If you can, you should hold your muscles tight both before and after the tube is removed and you are then shown to the toilet. If you cannot hold it do not worry, it sometimes leaks and it will only spill on to the paper covering on the floor. After this, you will then be taken back to the ward. You may expect to feel a little uncomfortable until your bowels are back to normal. This should take an hour or two, but you can eat and drink normally as soon as you want to. Your stools will be whitish for a day or two until all the barium is completely evacuated.

Fig. 2.1   Example of an explanation to patients

on their feelings pre-operatively and their progress post-operatively. The explanations were orientated to the patients viewpoint, what they would see, how it might feel, how long the pain would last, where the wound and dressing would be, what type of intravenous infusion would be likely and so on. Boore gave patients the opportunity to ask questions whenever they wished, and considered this was a necessary component of effective communication. She also allowed patients to ask for a repetition of any part of the explanation, and in general this seems to be a desirable policy whenever giving information to patients. The results of both these studies demonstrated that giving information was beneficial to the patients. Hayward's experimental group received less analgesia than the control group of patients. Boore's experimental group were found to have lower measures on physiological indicators of stress, such as urinary 17-hydroxycorticosteroid levels, and they also experienced fewer complications, such as wound infection, than the control group.

Although giving information has been associated with reduced anxiety and fewer physical signs of stress, the ways in which patients use this information remains something of a puzzle. A study by Andrew (1967) assessed the effect of giving patients careful pre-operative explanations of pre- and post-operative events. It was found that patients who received these explanations were less anxious, received less analgesia post-operatively, and recovered more quickly than others. However, they were unable to recall the information just after the operation.

There are numerous possible explanations for this puzzle. One is proposed in theories developed by Janis (1958). He suggested that patients use this type of information to prepare what is known as 'coping strategies' and to deal with difficult situations by 'rehearsing' for the forthcoming events. It may be that giving patients information means that they are simply less surprised when events occur, and can cope better with, say, pain or disfigurement. Each event during treatment or recovery should then jog their memory or reassure them, rather than setting them worrying about what will happen next.

Clearly, explanations and communication can work to reduce the patient's physical and psychological discomfort, and it is also clear that patients cope best when they know the truth. Therefore, nurses should honestly say when procedures will be painful, and patients should be told that doctors will expect them to say when they would like a rest or some analgesia.

Apart from pre-operative explanations it is also useful to employ a tactic which is termed 'positive appraisal'. Janis & Mann (1976) described this tactic as being another method of communication which gives the patient a way of coping with anxiety. When a patient expresses fear of an operation the nurse directs the patient's thoughts to the positive rewards which will result from facing this challenge, such as loss of the chronic pain or illness. When patients are despairing over post-operative discomfort the same applies, such as 'if you can just bear it for a couple of days, the pain will be gone for good.' This type of interaction is comforting for patients and is more useful than the platitudinous replies which all nurses are prone to utter at times when they feel rather inadequate.

Discharge from hospital   The patient's discharge from hospital is frequently rushed, particularly in surgical wards. Obviously, preparing patients for discharge one or two days prior to this event helps them to cope with their illness and life at home. Such preparation should include planning their convalescence, their continued medication, and other necessary advice including the ward's telephone number for contacting the staff 'whenever they wish'. Roberts (1975) found that general ward sisters ranked this sort of activity very low on their list of priorities, although they recognised that it could influence the patient's progress and reduce the likelihood of re-admission. It is important that staff should discuss patients' expected rate of rehabilitation and the problems of returning to work. The results of several research studies have demonstrated that a lack of this sort of communication from staff can lead to patients being discharged as 'psychological invalids'. For example, it has been shown that patients with heart conditions may be in particular need of realistic advice about rehabilitation and activity levels (Mayou et al. 1976).

Talking, listening and encouraging

Patients need to be talked to and listened to throughout their stay in hospital, but they also need less active kinds of company. A simple question like 'how are you feeling' helps the nurse to gauge whether conversation would be appreciated and whether she might encourage this by sitting down with the patient. However, many patients, while not wishing to be alone, are just too tired to talk, in which case the response might be 'would you prefer to sleep?' or 'shall I just sit here for a minute?'. At night, seriously ill patients often simply like to feel that someone is near. The ability to gauge this sort of need requires both sensitivity and experience on the part of the nurse, as she can often become the patient's friend and most constant source of support. This support may be helped if the nurse does things with the patient, like playing at cards or reading aloud. The resulting communication is a vital aspect of nursing care, and will often involve the nurse in sharing the patients' sorrows as well as their achievements. Such communication means a great deal to patients, and brings them comfort and support instead of loneliness.

Although important, empathy alone is often not enough. When a patient is due for rehabilitation he may need encouragement, helpful suggestions and practical hints which are just as essential in this situation as being an attentive and empathetic listener. The same principle can apply to what we call 'reassuring the patient'. Perhaps the most appropriate way to give reassurance is to provide the patients with a clear picture of their condition and what they can expect to happen. With this realistic basic knowledge they will be equipped to structure their activities inside and outside hospital. Patients are usually given little choice or responsibility during hospitalisation, and this can result in their feeling helpless and inferior. If they are supplied with adequate information, patients can feel part of a team and more responsible for their own recovery. For instance, if the nurse discusses the range of various aids, walking frames, orthopaedic corsets or even support stockings available to her patients, rather than leaving the appliances officer to order them, this can be rewarding for the nurse, allow the patient more involvement in his treatment and, perhaps most importantly, it usually leads to a more appropriate appliance!

Summary and conclusions

The information and suggestions made throughout this chapter have been based largely on research undertaken by nurses. Although the importance of non-verbal communication is acknowledged, the emphasis has been on verbal communication. This is because it was the explicit aim of the chapter to base the information given and suggestions made, wherever possible, on existing research evidence rather than on subjective opinion. In consequence, as very little research has been done in the area of non-verbal communication in nursing, less attention has been paid to this aspect in the chapter. Certainly, the research to date has demonstrated the value of talking and giving information to patients.

Nurses have greater opportunity than most other groups of staff for communicating with patients – indeed good communication is fundamental to the practice of nursing. We know that anxiety and other stress responses can impair health and it is important, therefore, to make every effort to reduce them. By anticipating patients' needs for knowledge and support at each stage of their stay in the general ward it is possible to help them to adjust appropriately.

Patients will not always feel the need for conversation with nurses, therefore nurses should learn to assess by verbal or non-verbal cues when patients need to talk. The characteristic nurses' 'bustle' can imply to patients that they are too busy to talk. Nurses' behaviour as well as their words must be geared to receiving and interpreting information from patients. Learning to listen and to spend time observing patients (and perhaps ourselves) is usually rewarding. Asking each nurse at report time 'How is your patient feeling?' or 'What is your patient's most important concern today?' usually reveals how little attention is devoted to patients' psychological needs. This kind of question from a senior nurse may do more than anything to emphasise this aspect of nursing care.

In order to communicate most effectively with patients it is suggested that nurses need to develop skills in the following areas.

1 Nurses should be able to recognise and help those patients who are in particular need of company. They should try to allow more time for conversation with patients, to become familiar with their particular needs and establish an easy rapport, so that patients can discuss their concerns when they feel this would be helpful.

2 Nurses need to develop their observational skills and increase their ability to empathise with patients by putting themselves into the patient's situation. In this way they will be better able to understand how he may be feeling, what he may like to know, or what could help him to cope with the future.

3 Nurses should be able to assess accurately any individual patient's need for information and be able to impart that information in an appropriate way.

Throughout our communication with patients we must give time to develop our skills as observers, assessors, listeners and informers and then examine our effectiveness through the benefits to our patients. This is not just a vague idea based on intangible evidence. Research has shown that improved nurse-patient communication does have measurable clinical and psychological benefits to patients.

References

Andrew J. M. (1967) *Coping Styles. Stress – Relevant to Learning and Recovery from Surgery.* Unpublished Ph.D. Thesis. Los Angeles: University of California

Boore J. (1979) *Prescription for Recovery.* London: RCN

Carnevali D. L. (1966) Preoperative anxiety. *American Journal of Nursing*, July, 1536–1538

Cartwright A. (1964) *Human Relations and Hospital Care.* London: Routledge & Kegan Paul

Coser R. L. (1965) Some functions of laughter. In J. K. Skipper & R. C. Leonard (eds) *Social Interaction and Patient Care.* Philadelphia: Lippincott, pp. 292–306

Elms R. R. & Leonard R. C. (1966) Effects of nursing approaches during admission. *Nursing Research*, **15** (winter), 39–48

Hayward J. C. (1975) *Information – A Prescription Against Pain.* London: RCN

Hockey L. (1976) *Women in Nursing.* Sevenoaks, Kent: Hodder & Stoughton

Hugh Jones P., Tanser A. R. & Whitby C. (1964) Patients view of admission to a London teaching hospital. *British Medical Journal*, **2** (12 Sept.), 660–664

Janis I. L. (1958) *Psychological Stress.* New York: John Wiley

Janis I. L. & Mann L. (1976) Coping with decisional conflict. *American Scientist*, **64** (Nov–Dec), 657–667

Johnson J. E., Morrisey J. F. & Leventhal H. (1973) Psychological preparation for an endoscopic examination. *Gastrointestinal Endoscopy*, **19** (4), 180–182

Kubler Ross E. (1969) *On Death and Dying.* New York: MacMillan Publishing Co

Maguire P. G. (1978) The psychological effects of cancer and their treatments. In R. Tiffany (ed) *Oncology for Nurses, Vol 2*. London: Allen & Unwin

Mayou R., Williamson B. & Foster A. (1976) Attitudes and advice after myocardial infarction. *British Medical Journal*, **1**, 1577–9

Menzies I. E. (1960) A case study on the functioning of social systems as a defence against anxiety. A report of the nursing service in a general hospital. *Human Relations*, November, 13–32

Moffic H. S. & Paykel E. S. (1975) Depression in medical inpatients. *British Journal of Psychiatry*, **126**, 346–352

Raphael W. (1969) *Patients and their Hospitals*. King Edward's Hospital Fund for London

Rhys Hearn C. (1968) How many high care patients? *Nursing Times*, **14**, 504–505

Roberts I. (1975) *Discharge From Hospital*. Study of Nursing Care Series London: RCN

Siminov L. (1970) In M. Arnold (ed). *Feelings and Emotions*. New York: Academic Press

Stockwell F. (1972) *The Unpopular Patient*. London: RCN

Wilson-Barnett J. (1977) *Patients' Emotional Reactions to Hospitalisation*. PhD Thesis, University of London

Wilson-Barnett J. (1978) Patients' emotional responses to barium X-rays. *Journal of Advanced Nursing*, **3**, 37–46

Wilson-Barnett J. & Carrigy A. (1978) Factors affecting patients' responses to hospitalisation. *Journal of Advanced Nursing*, **3**, 221–228

Chapter 3: Communicating with Children in Hospital

In this chapter we move from examining general principles of communicating with the wide range of adult patients on general wards to investigating the very specific communication needs of children in hospital. Being admitted to hospital will inevitably be stressful for children. The rapid developmental changes that take place in childhood, and the large individual differences in their ability and comprehension all mean that a nurse caring for sick children must be skilled, highly sensitive and flexible in her approach to communication.

However, it is impossible to think of the child's needs without also being aware of those of the parents and the family. Therefore, readers will find two recurring themes in this chapter:

> *the importance of effective communication in meeting both the children's emotional needs and those of the parents*

> *the needs of the parents and the family in paediatric nursing, and their role in caring for and communicating with their own sick child.*

This chapter contains a variety of suggestions and accounts of communication in paediatrics which arise from the author's personal experience. Many practical and imaginative ideas are given for increasing nurses' ability to communicate with young patients and their families – ideas which can be tried by every nurse who is involved with caring for children.

June Jolly qualified initially as a social worker specialising in child care. She later did her SRN training at St Thomas' Hospital, London, and since that time has had considerable experience working with sick children both as a ward sister and nursing officer. She has travelled widely over Canada and the USA on a Florence Nightingale scholarship, studying family involvement and innovative care in paediatrics. Since returning to the UK she has written many articles and lectured widely on these aspects of paediatric care. As a result, in recent years several of the new ideas she observed have been implemented in paediatric units in a number of British general hospitals.

Chapter 3

Communicating with Children in Hospital

June Jolly

Introduction

The nursing of children is demanding. It can be frustrating and stressful, it can be exhausting, and it can be fun. One of the great differences between nursing children and most other patients lies in the area of communication. Children can be devastatingly frank, but they can just as easily be totally confused by what they see and hear. Young children often cannot tell what is wrong, often cannot identify pain, and may come to some surprising conclusions about the treatment they receive. Children need to be simply and truthfully prepared for their stay in hospital as well as for any treatment they are given. Much of this preparation will involve the parents, and in any communication with sick children, parents need to be just as well informed.

As long ago as the 1920's the practice of mothers living in hospital with their babies was advocated. There is now worldwide acknowledgement of the work of Spence (1947), Bowlby (1953), Robertson (1956) and others in highlighting the potential damage caused by separating young children from their mothers. Twenty years ago the Platt Report (Ministry of Health 1959) laid down guidelines for the care and welfare of children in hospital which apparently still have not been implemented right across the country. Indeed, Hawthorn (1974) showed that even in wards where adequate children's staff are available, the children are liable to be lonely and desolate.

The presence and involvement of parents is essential in all aspects of care. For example, MaCarthy (1974) pointed out the misunderstandings that can arise in out-patient sessions if parents are excluded. Even where parents have been well briefed and have good rapport with their children, their presence in hospital does not reduce the need for the nurses to communicate meaningfully with their young patients or the parents.

Some interesting work has been carried out in the USA on communication with sick children. Plank (1971) pioneered the use of outline diagrams of the child's body on which could be drawn the faulty organs whilst explanations were given about what the doctors were going to do. These were designed for use in out-patient sessions by the doctor as well as in the ward. Petrillo *et al.* (1972) showed that nurses using rag dolls, on which stitches could be sewn or catheters and tubes attached, were able to explain procedures to children in a way which was much easier for them to understand. She also demonstrated the value of using syringes and needles for supervised play sessions. This work has influenced practice in progressive paediatric units throughout the United States amongst medical, nursing and other disciplines concerned with sick children. It seems a pity that these techniques are not better known in this country, particularly among medical staff who tend to find it difficult to explain surgical and other procedures to parents and children in a way that can be understood. This apparent lack of interest in such research is reflected in the fact that although more staff here appear to acknowledge the child's need for unlimited visiting, very few attempts are made to meet the other emotional needs of the young patient, particularly in the area of communication. What is accomplished by way of improvements in communication with children in UK hospitals is mostly intuitive and unstructured, and thus it often goes unrecognised.

Needs of specific age groups

There are some needs which virtually all children share; others are applicable only to certain ages, and some needs are specific to well-defined groups of children. Obviously, a child's rate of development and understanding will be influenced by many factors besides his chronological age and, under a stress such as a hospital experience, it is to be expected that the child will behave less maturely than under normal circumstances.

For children, being in hospital will be a time of learning and new experiences. Children often find it easier both to learn and to express themselves through playing games such as 'let's pretend', dressing up and painting. Telling, watching, practising, and playing are all methods which can be used easily on the wards. Staff need some basic facts, both about children's ability to understand things, and about the ages at which certain things become important to children. To be aware of the words individual children generally use for things like urination, defaecation, the penis, and so on, and knowing the names of the rest of the child's family, their special comforter, and any routine they have at bedtime, will help to provide a framework from which to plan nursing care. I have divided children's needs into four broad categories. Although each one could be further subdivided and is characterised by specific needs, children's maturity seems to vary so much that I have found it unnecessary to categorise those over one year too closely for this purpose.

Children under three   The infant and toddler stage is when the child is almost entirely dependent on a 'significant adult' for care and well-being, and his ability to communicate verbally is very limited. Children under three are emotionally unable to relate to adults except as to a 'Mother.' Even toddlers who well understand what the family says may be quite unable to understand the same thing from a stranger because the accompanying expressions and tone of voice are unfamiliar. Thus a nurse or any other outsider starts off at a great disadvantage with children in this age group. Ideally, the nurse should work through the mother, or at any rate alongside her. Even children under two years of age may understand a simple explanation, but it needs to be in visual terms; for example, a dressing procedure can be shown by bandaging a teddy bear. If a child of this age needs to be put in traction, it is now policy in the more progressive units to prepare them gradually over several days, wherever possible, by putting on leg bandages the first day, then attaching them loosely to the end of the cot for a while before applying traction.

A child of two has little concept of the past or future. To console him with 'never mind, Mummy will be here tomorrow!' will be small comfort and to say 'she will be back tomorrow afternoon!' is likely to mean nothing. 'After lunch!' or 'After you have had a sleep!' may have more meaning, as it identifies with something tangible the child can understand. If parents leave a glove, handbag, or something else recognised by the youngster, this will help assure the child that they will come back. Fear of abandonment is real for the toddler whose separation from mother can have no other meaning to him.

Even for much older children the fear of being 'lost' from one's parents is a nightmarish possibility. I have known children of nine or ten express fear that their parents will not be able to find them just because their bed has been moved to another part of the same ward. One four year old who I thought had understood and wanted 'a little room, all of her own' was distraught on being moved and sobbed 'now ... Mummy ... not ... find me!'.

Children of four to seven   Children of about this age are more wordly-wise and adventurous, but still need a great deal of 'intimate parenting'. Children under seven also often have a lively imagination and an active fantasy life. Three- and four-year olds, in particular, play with imaginary playmates, so including such playmates in a conversation can help to gain an accurate picture of a child who cannot express thoughts or feelings himself. Dolls and teddys can be profitably brought into service too. At this age, when children are newly aware of themselves, the body assumes great importance. The fear of losing any part of their body, however small, can be devastating. The well-known fear of castration in boys undergoing circumcision is a case in point. Children of this age need frequent reassurance that damage to one part of their body does not mean that other parts will be affected.

Children over seven   This is a more independent and resilient age group whose members gain increasing support from other children of their own age, and sometimes show little interest in adult advice. Children over seven may suffer as much during hospitalisation as younger children, but the cause may be somewhat different. They may continue to be very dependent on their parents, but their concerns will be becoming more orientated to other children of their own age, and the 'peer group's' ways and attitudes are increasingly important. This is the age of great physical energy and much of a child's feelings are expressed in energetic running around. When a boy of this age is confined to bed with a fractured femur, for example, he has little or no way of discharging his feelings, and may well express his frustration in belligerent or depressed behaviour. Children like this can benefit from being provided with outlets for their energy, such as having a punchball hung above or beside the bed.

Adolescents   Adolescence is a no-man's land; an insecure time when many youngsters oscillate from demanding adult freedom of choice to dependence on adults for support when the going gets tough. As adolescence approaches, the young patient may become self-conscious and worried about his body. He may cover up his fear of the future or his prognosis by means of anti-social behaviour. Irritation and intolerance of 'fussy' parents may hide his wish for their presence. Often the pain and anxiety of separation is just as real as with the younger children, and as with younger children, one cannot expect an adolescent to explain his anxieties and fears to an adult without 'testing' the adult first to be sure that he will be taken seriously and considerately. For adolescents, the fear of being thought silly, being laughed at or teased can be intolerable.

Establishing communication with children

How does one communicate? Certainly not only by the words which are spoken. In fact, words can be so misleading for children that they *must* be chosen with care. To approach a child with some medicine saying 'Will you take this for me?' invites the child to answer the question '. . . No'. In general, I find that 'Will you?' or 'May I? . . .' should be used only rarely. If there is no choice, then do not imply one. When talking about a surgical procedure be careful not to use the words 'Take out' or 'Cut off . . .' as this may imply a much more drastic or frightening prospect to a child than was ever intended. To replace such words with the doctor will 'Fix it' . . .' 'Mend it' or 'Repair it . . .' hold fewer connotations of pain or mutilation and yet are understood by most children.

Children's descriptions of being in hospital, or even their drawings about it, show how easily they can misinterpret things which are said to them, or magnify them out of all proportion. It is for this reason that in some hospitals where children are regularly prepared for surgical intervention a senior nurse is designated for this task. In some places, experienced play workers undertake this role as they have good rapport with the children and are often better educated in the principles of communication and child development. However, this in no way excuses the nurse from playing an active part in preparing her young patients but she may need to learn new skills.

In hospital, children often get upset, and sometimes they cry. Unhappiness is something that the nurse often interprets as failure on her part, and she immediately attempts to distract the child and cheer him up. When this fails she may well abandon the scene, and the crying then turns to sobbing until the child falls asleep, exhausted. Sadly, unhappiness, home-sickness and discomfort are inevitable parts of a stay in hospital. It is not necessary, however, to leave a child comfortless. A cuddle and a listening ear will do wonders. When a child is struggling bravely not to cry, try gently but persistently talking about home, his family, his feelings about hospital − whatever may be causing the anguish. The relief to the child is nearly always apparent after he has been shown that it is all right to have a really good cry.

Children in hospital see a great deal more than the staff suppose.

Jill, a 4-year-old tracheotomy patient, greeted me one morning on the ward 'Did you know a baby died last night?' 'Yes' I nodded. 'It died in there' Jill continued, pointing to the bathroom (the staff had been sure everyone was asleep when it had occurred). 'Oh!' I countered (hoping Jill would tell me more). Jill then asked 'Did they kill it in there?' I explained 'No one killed the baby, Jill, the baby died because it wasn't strong enough to breathe any more.' Jill added 'I was like that once wasn't I? . . . but I was too strong!'

If I had been too quick to reply or had attempted an explanation earlier it might never have been possible to correct Jill's thinking.

When a five-year-old boy died unexpectedly on one of the children's wards I made it my business to go round the ward talking to all the children and parents. It seemed important that everyone should know and not be left with possibly distorted ideas of what had happened. Asking what they had seen helped me to know how much each individual needed to be told. One ten-year-old described in detail the efforts at resuscitation. Asked how he had seen it he explained it had been reflected in the window opposite his bed. (We had made sure the scene had been well screened.) Rather than being terrified the boy said it made him want to get out of bed and help, too!

One little girl being taken to theatre well pre-medicated was waiting for admission to the anaesthetic room which was adjacent to the recovery ward, where loud screams could be heard. Looking at the child I could not decide whether she even heard them. 'Do you hear that child crying?' I ventured when she opened her eyes momentarily. 'Yes . . . es' she replied with great feeling. 'It's Diane, she's had her tonsils out and wants to go back to the ward', I explained. I noticed that Lynne visibly sank back into the stretcher, although I had been totally unaware of how rigidly she had been lying before we spoke.

It can never be assumed that children have not seen or heard everything that is going on in the ward, nor can it be assumed that they will come to an adult's conclusion about what they have seen. There are no short cuts to giving sensitive, observant attention, and listening to a child's version if we are to be sure of communicating facts about hospital life.

Preparing children for hospital

Over 30% of children in Britain spend at least one night in hospital before they are seven. According to one survey in south-east London (1976), 61% of all child admissions were emergencies and over 85% of children admitted for medical reasons came into this category. It is not hard to see that in a majority of cases there is little or no prospect of having time to prepare a child for going into hospital. Most preparation must, therefore, come under the heading of education. Time spent with groups even of small children waiting to go to hospital may be time well spent if they are shown the things they might see as patients – the bedside locker, the bed table to eat or play on, the unfamiliar 'bottle' and 'bedpan', curtains that pull round beds, and the nurse who stays awake all night in case anyone wakes up. These things are so simple that we forget they are totally alien to the child's experience. Puppets dressed in hospital uniforms, the judicious use of pictures, slides and books can also help. Doctors' and nurses' outfits are always popular, and slides and videotapes are also being used in a few hospitals for children awaiting admission in accident and emergency, or out-patient departments.

Most ENT patients and those awaiting 'cold' surgery are not admitted as emergencies. One of the easiest ways of preparing such children is to invite them beforehand to visit the ward and meet the staff. Booklets produced by individual hospitals and the National Association for the Welfare of Children in Hospital (NAWCH)* help by giving the child and parent some idea of what to expect. A

*NAWCH: Exton House, 7 Exton Street, London SE1

simple duplicated leaflet addressed to the child himself and included with the admission information can convey a warm invitation to find out what goes on in the hospital. In some larger paediatric units it is possible to provide an organised tour and a demonstration, perhaps using puppets, to spell out the admission procedure. Details of treatments, operations and so on are better left until a relationship has been established with the child. But it is important to stress to children that they will have to sleep in hospital and to highlight things that will be different from home. For example, if the children have breakfast in bed, or supper in their pyjamas, it is good to point this out. The Children's Hospital in Washington, DC, have a superb puppet script which they use for pre-admission parties and this could be easily adapted for British audiences.

Involving health visitors in preparing young children and their parents for admission is useful, too, as they should already have good relationship with the parents, and know the family circumstances. Whenever possible, liaison with health visitors before, during, and after in-patient treatment ensures continuity of physical care, and the best opportunity for psychological support. Where such a relationship exists with the local hospitals, there is much less chance that inaccurate or out-of-date information will be relayed to the parents or the child.

Preparing children for treatment
We have seen the difficulty of getting hold of children at times to prepare them for coming into hospital. Once in the ward, children are often subjected to so many tests and procedures that there is hardly a time when communication is not vital. The difficulty lies in helping the young patient to understand what is going to happen, and to show him how it is going to help. We need to be alert for new and frightening experiences for each child, and ready to step in in time to support him through it. The amount of preparation given will depend on the age of the child. For major surgery or treatment, a good rule is to start general preparation one day before admission for each year of the child's age, ie. three days before admission for a 3-year-old; a week for a 7-year-old. Specific preparation need not begin until the day before unless the child is anxious, and it is best not to tell children about injections or 'pricks' until they are about to be given, but then do admit it will hurt for a minute.

We all learn by hearing, seeing and then practising. Children, we are told, learn by 'playing', and much of this playing is in fact 'practising'. By using simple language and familiar vocabulary it is possible to explain what the treatment will involve. It is important to concentrate once again on those things that the child will notice, such as an unexpected bath, or wearing a 'gown' (which could be described as a 'shirt put on backwards', or a 'nightie split down the back'). Deprivation of a meal, for example, is of far more interest to most children than checking the pre-med, or the time of scheduled surgery. The child will want to know that the doctor has a special medicine to help him go to sleep, or repair the ailing part. I have found that patients of all ages are apprehensive of actually getting to sleep and then staying asleep throughout the operation. 'Magic' sleep satisfies most of the under-eights. Older ones are often preoccupied with whether they will have a 'needle' or 'blow up the bag', and most anaesthetists are happy to co-operate if a child has a preference.

It is good to follow-up explanations by demonstrations. Borrowed theatre trolleys and gowns make good props, and give children and parents a chance to try things out in a less tense atmosphere. At the same time it is helpful to try to discover the child's own concept of what is to happen to him, and how the doctor will do it, so that the correct explanations can be understood. For example, some children really think the doctor has to slit their throats in order to get at their tonsils; similarly, I once nursed a child due for insertion of a Spitz-Holter valve who drew the most detailed picture of a surgeon operating on a completely severed head. Clear explanations, and proper communication may be essential for the child's recovery.

> Robert, aged eight, had been in hospital before for a fractured femur and did not appear to mind being re-admitted some months later for the removal of the plate. All went well until post-operatively. No amount of persuasion could get this active little boy back onto his feet. Eventually we realised that he did not really trust the judgment of the surgeon as he could not imagine how his leg could be strong enough without the plate. Although he did not volunteer this information he did admit that was how he felt. By looking at the series of X-rays together he could 'see' how much stronger his leg had become. With his confidence restored there were no more complaints that he would not get up – only that he was a nuisance tearing round the ward!

It is easy to 'show' children about plaster casts and stitches, and they all enjoy helping to apply miniature versions to a doll. A number of hospitals keep a supply of rag dolls made by local volunteers for just this purpose and even the child undergoing intravenous therapy, EEGs, ECGs, or surgery of any sort can be shown what happens and why. Both boys and girls seem to like to keep their dolls, and they often demand that the stitches are taken out of the doll first!

One hospital I visited in the United States used this sort of doll most successfully in their burns unit. The children cut out the area on the doll corresponding to their own injury, and thereafter this was patched with gauze. Before discharge the young patients sewed back the original piece of 'skin'. In the meantime the dolls accompanied the children through all their treatments, baths, and so on, and proved to be an excellent medium for communication. Another real-life example of how a doll can provide invaluable help is given here:

> Diane, aged six, had an emergency appendicectomy: 36 hours later she remained monosyllabic, flushed and withdrawn. The doctor feared an abscess and she was booked for an X-ray. She denied any pain but showed a spark of interest when we suggested that we might tell her what had happened after she came to the hospital as she said she didn't know.
>
> Using a doll to show her, she quickly became animated, and had definite ideas as to how many stitches dolly needed. Despite what seemed real mutilation of the doll in the process, she declared it didn't hurt her at all. Only when the doll was complete with a Kleenex dressing and a plaster applied by Diane did she announce dolly felt sore. 'Is that how your tummy feels, too?' 'Yes,' she nodded. Within hours of this conversation Diane's condition improved. The understanding registrar addressed all his subsequent conversation with Diane through the doll. And of course taking out dolly's stitches first allayed Diane's anxiety about this procedure.

Not all preparation is that easy, and preparing children for procedures like enucleation of the eye, amputation, or hair loss can be difficult and distressing. For the five- and six-year-olds especially, mutilation or loss of a limb can constitute a real threat to their identity and survival. Petrillo et al. (1972) describe graphically just how important it is to a child and his parents to come to some sort of understanding prior to major surgery, but it is difficult to know what to do about the young inarticulate child, the pre-schooler, or the toddler whose experience is limited to his family and home. The nurse's first reaction may be that there is no point in bothering to try to explain things to them. For example, imagine the difficulties of nursing a two-year-old child who wakes up bewildered and, in isolation, to find that his hands and feet have totally vanished under huge occlusive dressings. She may stand in anguish as the child retreats further and further into himself, knowing that verbal explanation is useless, as the child does not have a wide enough vocabulary to comprehend. Stories involving the injury repeated over and over again may help, but the most successful way of getting through to the child is through demonstration, such as by bandaging teddy's hands and feet, undoing them saying 'See, teddy's hand is still there'. Repeated many times, this can be a game, but is also reassuring for the child. Similar games can be played with children with congenital dislocation of hip, for example, and several four- and five-year-olds I know are the proud mums of dolls with Spitz-Holter valves which they delight to demonstrate.

Hospital equipment – gowns, masks, stethoscopes, spatulae, medicine glasses and bandages make excellent props, as does the coveted syringe, and they give rise to surprising but exciting dramatisations of a child's-eye view. Some hospitals run regular play sessions with such equipment to which they add willing members of staff as patients. The turning of a Wendy House into a hospital gives added scope to children playing on their own. When it is not clear whether the pre-school child has understood why he is in hospital, and what is going to be done, playing doctors and nurses on the toy telephone often reveals what the child really thinks, and it is relatively easy to correct inaccuracies if it is the nurse who is on one end of the phone!

Communicating with parents

No communication with sick children can be really effective unless the family is well informed, whether this is father and mother or the 'significant carer' to whom the child looks for security and love. When a child is in hospital his family is under great strain, and they often wonder about what is actually wrong, and whose fault it was. Explanations by professionals, be they doctors, nurses or social workers are often hidden in a mass of jargon. Not only does communication suffer through misunderstanding of technical language, but parents are so emotionally involved that they only hear a portion of what is said, and yet are reluctant to show their ignorance by asking questions.

It is important to make time to listen to parents, and unravel their interpretations of what has been said. This is often coloured by the parents' own previous hospital experiences. Even when the consultant includes parents on his round, and takes pains to explain to them what is being done, I have found that it is important for someone to stay behind and re-iterate in simple terms what has just been said. The parents may not have understood or have needed time to formulate questions of importance. It is imperative therefore that the senior nurse understands exactly what the doctor has told the patient and relatives so that no confusion arises. The nurse can then translate the doctor's explanations into everyday examples which the parents will understand. One example is to use the analogy of weighing scales in order to illustrate the need to balance food and insulin for a diabetic, and another compares pyloric stenosis to a type of elastic band round the outlet of the stomach. Everyday language may appear unprofessional, but it can be enormously reassuring to anxious parents and greatly enhance communication between staff and parents.

Any nurse who has had experience of parents in hospital with their young children knows that sometimes parents can be belligerent, aggressive, and occasionally abusive! The parents may complain that everything is wrong; care is not being given on time; the child has been left in a wet bed; he has been sick, and so on. It is so easy for the nurse to over-react to this and become defensive. Sometimes a scapegoat is found, but it is important to stand back and recognise the enormous strain that is on parents of sick children. Making time to listen will often involve listening through the superficial grievances – until one hears the parents' real anxiety which is often due simply to failure of communication.

Infants and neonates

Only in the last few years has much attention or research been directed towards the emotional needs of this very early age group. The establishment of initial mother-infant bonding has been described by Klaus & Kennel (1976) and is now increasingly recognised as vital in child development. Special Care Baby Units (SCBU) tend to vary from highly technological 'baby laboratories' full of expensive equipment connected to minute bodies whose features are distorted by huge eye masks at one extreme, to warm nurseries where sleeping babies are snugly tucked in their cribs resting for a few hours or days after a traumatic delivery at the other extreme. To introduce new and anxious parents into the latter can be re-assuring, to the former an awful experience which needs careful and continued explanation and support. Nevertheless, the importance of establishing a relationship or bond between parent and child is increasingly being recognised, even within the intensive care setting of the SBCU.

The introduction of colour, music and comfortable nursing chairs beside the cribs and incubators helps to establish an atmosphere in which parents can feel free to begin to get to know their own baby. Wherever the physical conditions allow, the tube feeding can be administered whilst the mother cuddles the baby.

It is not only in the SCBUs that special facilities for parents need to be provided. Once a baby and mother are transferred to the paediatric unit the situation often dramatically alters. Whilst visitors maybe allowed to come and go more freely, the mother's own needs may be given scant attention. Yet it is just at this time that she may need much support in getting to know and handle her baby. It is amazing how few nurses and mothers speak to, or look at their infants. Talking, crooning, and stroking are vital ways of establishing contact with children in their early days of life. The confidence and sureness with which a baby is handled and held can communicate itself just as surely as tucking a baby warmly into his crib and establishing eye-to-eye contact with him. Adults know the importance of holding a person's hand, especially when they are fearful or weak, and many young parents find holding their baby's hand through the incubator porthole just as reassuring. Research suggests they also benefit.

Terminally-ill children

If ever there is a time when the nurse needs to be aware of children's ability to sense the feelings and anxieties of adults, it is when she is caring for a child with a fatal illness. It is important to remember that it is not only parents and relatives who transmit this atmosphere. Staff on a children's ward are perhaps always more affected by an impending death than on other types of ward. This applies to all members of the ward team and there would seem to be something deeply rooted in human nature that makes us resent death at the beginning of life. If communication is to be maintained between adult and child, the adult will need both strength of character and support. In some units, the member of staff who has the best rapport with a dying child is given charge of his care, but she is supported in the background by the other members of the ward team.

The family need to be included, too. Children do see life and death issues in their own inimitable way. The younger child particularly may be more concerned with the superficial side-effects of his illness than with the impending separation or fear of dying, but older children often become withdrawn and uncommunicative. It can never be assumed that any child will view death as adults do, or for the same reasons. I knew one seven-year-old who tried to comfort his distraught and rather verbose mother by saying 'I don't mind being invisible you know, don't be upset'. And a two-year-old said in my presence 'Mummy not worry, I'se all right' – this was on the day she died after a prolonged fight with a rhabdomyosarcoma. Just as adults need pain control, children can be enabled to enjoy their life and their games until shortly before they die by the regular and judicious use of analgesics, preferably of the diamorphine group so they are not too sleepy.

The parents' problems often cause the family alternatively to pamper and withdraw from a doomed child. For example, if a remission occurs, the immediate family may relax into normality but other relatives may continue to behave as if death is imminent. The family will need to know that staff understand and are with them, and prepared to talk and listen. As a long vigil comes to an end with a slowly-dying, comatose child, the parents may need support and reassurance as they start withdrawing emotionally from their child. When nursing terminally-ill children, as with all others, the value of listening cannot be overstated. MaCarthy (1974) emphasised that it is not always easy to have the patience to listen to children, it being much easier to fill in the gaps, or finish the sentence for them. Asking questions that can have a YES or NO for answer are good conversation stoppers and reveal nothing of the child's feelings. When a child asks a question or makes a statement, try turning it round, and instead of answering, reply with a questioning tone 'That's how you feel about it, is it?'. Be sure to wait long enough for them to continue.

Research by Bluebond-Langer (1978) has shown that children do go through recognised stages as death approaches. From her work it would seem that they pick up a great deal from their parents' attitudes, even when nothing is actually said. In the absence of a religious experience on the part of the parents, the child is unlikely to be satisfied by talk of a vague 'heaven' or 'being with Jesus'. On the other hand, those with a real faith are often able to make this tragic situation into a positive and growing experience for the whole family. Staff must know where they stand individually if they are to be of any help to children or their families in these circumstances. Children always ferret out insincerity and truth. Even if you have to say that you don't know about some aspect of death, it is essential to be honest if you want to build up any relationship of trust with children.

Summary

Communication with children is a challenge and involves all the facilities and skills at the nurses' disposal. Verbal communication alone is never enough and needs to be linked with visual and practical demonstration and involvement with the child. Areas of particular concern will include the child's admission, treatment and investigations. Communication needs to be two-way and children need the opportunity to express their feelings and begin to understand what is happening to them. Parents cannot be left out as, for the younger child in particular, they constitute an integral part of the child's world.

Despite the devastating effect on a child of any separation from home, a hospitalisation can, and should be a learning experience. The child's development may be temporarily slowed down or changed, but it need not cease. Children can emerge much richer and more mature, having developed their resources to cope with adverse circumstances. To a large measure this enrichment will depend on the nurses' ability to anticipate and meet the emotional, and psychological needs of the child as well as his physical needs.

As staff dedicated to the care and development of children, we cannot ignore our duty to improve communication with our patients while we still find children saying:

> 'The doctors looked at my throat, they looked at my ears, they looked at my tummy, but they didn't look at ME!' (*Johnnie, aged five*)
>
> 'My name is not 'Hey You', my name is not 'little boy', my name is ANDRE!' (*Andre, aged eight*)
>
> In answer to 'what is it like in hospital?' *Kathy, aged thirteen*, said 'It's like being lonesome all the time!'

Nothing can take the place of human contact. Each sick child is an individual, and has the right to be treated with respect, which demands that we care enough to listen to what is being said to us. We need to get alongside each young patient and his parents as they struggle with hospital and sickness, but we also need the ability and determination to interpret the truth in love.

References

Bluebond-Langner M. (1978) *The Private Worlds of Dying Children.* Princeton University Press

Bowlby J. (1953) *Child Care and the Growth of Love.* Harmondsworth: Penguin Books

Hawthorn P. (1974) *Nurse I Want my Mummy.* London: RCN

Jolly J. (1976) *Home Care for Sick Children.* Greenwich and Bexley AHA Unpublished Report

Klaus N. H. & Kennel J. H. (1976) *Mother/Infant Bonding.* St Louis, Mo.: Mosby

MaCarthy D. (1974) Between children and doctors. *Developmental Medicine & Child Neurology*, 6(3), 279–285

Ministry of Health (1959) *The Platt Report: Welfare of Children in Hospital.* London: HMSO

Petrillo M. & Sanger S. (1972) *Emotional Care of the Hospitalised Child.* Philadelphia: Lippincott

Pilliteri A. *et al.* (1977) *Nursing Care of the Growing Family.* Boston: Little, Brown

Plank E. (1971) *Working with Children in Hospitals.* Chicago: Case Western Reseserve/Year Book Medical Publishers

Robertson J. (1956) *Young Children in Hospital.* London: Tavistock Publications

Spence J. C. (1947) Care of children in hospital. *British Medical Journal*, **1**, 5–30

Suggested further reading

Bergmann T. & Freud A. (1965) *Children in Hospital*. New York: International Universities Press

Blake F. G. (1954) *The Child, His Parents and the Nurse*. Philadelphia: Lippincott

Burton L. (1974) *The Care of the Child Facing Death*. London: Routledge & Kegan Paul

Burton L. (1975) *The Family Life of Sick Children*. London: Routledge & Kegan Paul

Donaldson M (1978) *Children's Minds*. Glasgow: Fontana

Hardgrove C. & Dawson R. (1972) *Parents and Children in Hospital*. Boston: Little, Brown

Leach P. (1977) *Baby and Child*. London: Michael Joseph

Noble E. (1967) *Play and the Sick Child*. London: Faber & Faber

Solnit A. J. & Green M. (1963) *The Paediatric Management of the Dying Child. Part II: The Child's Reaction to Dying. Modern Perspectives in Child Development*. New York: International Universities Press, pp. 217–228

Vernon D. *et al. The Psychological Responses of Children to Hospitalisation and Illness*. Illinios: Charles C. Thomas

Chapter 4: Communicating with Geriatric Patients

This chapter looks at the communication needs of a further large group of patients with whom all nurses have some contact, namely the elderly. Nurses working with the elderly meet patients who have a wide range of physical and mental abilities, and this chapter demonstrates how the individual communication needs of geriatric patients can be met. Some of these communication needs are specific to the elderly, while others are shared with other groups of patients discussed in other chapters. For example, as in intensive care and paediatrics, many elderly patients will be highly dependent and, in addition, communicating with the family or relatives will be an important part of the nurses' role.

The fact that the population of old people is growing means that every nurse will have increasing contact with elderly patients either in general wards, geriatric units or in the community. This chapter therefore examines some of the problems or barriers that nurses may encounter when communicating with geriatric patients, and the author describes a number of strategies for reducing these problems.

Growing emphasis is being placed on keeping elderly patients active in the community both through rehabilitation programmes and through other attempts to preserve and increase each patient's independence. In order to achieve this aim it is essential that physical care is combined with effective communication. Examples from research evidence are given which suggest that the importance of relationships and interactions between nurses and geriatric patients is often overlooked. Encouraging such patients to become, or remain, independent means that nurses must *possess specific and appropriate communication skills.*

There can be little doubt that communicating with patients who are confused, depressed or even demented presents enormous problems, especially if there are additional physical barriers of poor hearing or sight to overcome. Simple and practical suggestions are made to show how nurses can begin to overcome these barriers, and in this context the role of non-verbal communication between nurses and patients is emphasised. The ways in which nurses' attitudes can affect the quality of care given are also discussed, and the author highlights the need for all nurses to look critically at their own attitudes and to become more aware of how they approach and care for their elderly patients.

The author of this chapter, Pauline Fielding, gained her SRN at the Bury and Fairfield School of Nursing. She worked for some time in a geriatric unit as a nurse researcher before taking a degree in psychology. She is currently involved in further research in which she is investigating student nurses' attitudes to geriatric nursing and aspects of how nurses actually communicate with geriatric patients on the wards.

Chapter 4

Communicating with Geriatric Patients

Pauline Fielding

Introduction

Growing old is a normal part of life, and an increasing number of people are surviving to experience old age. In 1901, nearly 2 million people in Britain were aged over 65, compared with a total of 8 million today, and by 1986 there will be a further 24% increase in the population over 75 years of age (DHSS 1978). If the nursing profession is to meet society's needs, there will clearly be a growing need for nurses to specialise in the care of the elderly. This fact has been recognised by the General Nursing Council, since experience in geriatric nursing is now included in all nurse training schemes.

There is no clear line to be drawn between the 'normal' ageing process and various disease processes. There are, however, wide differences in ability and state of health between individuals of the same age. Indeed, a person's chronological age can be a poor indicator of his state of health. The ageing process may be accelerated by a number of pathological processes and, in general, degenerative diseases develop more rapidly in the old. This is one reason why communication between nurses and geriatric patients is very important. The ability to make personal contact, provide support and give advice are essential skills which can help elderly patients to cope with their problems and avoid institutionalisation. In general, it has been suggested that knowledge of communication may be more pertinent to nursing than knowledge of disease (Smith 1964) and this is especially true in geriatric nursing where the nurse-patient relationship should represent the foundation of all aspects of care – a foundation on which all other treatments, plans, and procedures can be built.

Much of what has been written on communicating with geriatric patients is diverse, vague, and largely prescriptive in nature. Most of the books and articles do not deal specifically with nurses and geriatric patients, but look at the communication difficulties of the elderly at a more general level. One example is an article by Bloom *et al.* (1971) which considers problem areas for the elderly such as limitations of hearing, vision, and language. These authors also describe the effects of pain and fatigue upon communication by the elderly, and suggest ways in which communication can be dealt with in such situations.

In order to communicate effectively, it is necessary to use verbal and non-verbal channels. A great deal of information is transmitted both through what is said and how it is said. Several researchers have examined the kind of communication that takes place between nurses and geriatric patients. However, most have looked closely at *either* the verbal *or* the non-verbal aspects of the communication. The background research is therefore discussed under these two headings.

Non-verbal communication   Geriatric patients are often depressed or inarticulate, and Blazer (1978) emphasises the importance of looking for non-verbal cues in the patients' facial expressions and gestures which communicate their feelings of depression and anxiety far more clearly than their words ever can. Non-verbal communication is clearly an essential element of communication with elderly patients, and this has been the subject of a number of research studies. Burnside (1973), DeWever (1977) and McCorkle (1974) have investigated the use and meaning of touch as a tech-

Table 4.1.   Classification of the content of nurse-patient verbal communication (Wells 1980, p.115)

Content category	Percentage frequency	Percentage duration	Principal activity of nurse
Procedural	54·1	35·9	Physical care tasks Instructing/ explaining Encouraging Orientating
Mixed procedural	25·0	51·7	Physical care tasks
Personal	20·8	12·2	Physical care tasks Socialising

nique for communication in nursing, and as an alternative to talking when words are inappropriate or impossible.

They found that adults respond in various ways to being touched depending upon their age, upbringing, culture and, not least, on who is touching them. Some patients were found to appreciate a simple and warm gesture, like a hand placed on the shoulder, whilst for others, this kind of non-verbal communication made them feel uncomfortable. Nurses also reacted differently to physical contact with patients, but in general it seems likely that the absence of touching as a deliberate technique for communication with elderly patients may be more of an example of 'British reserve' than any kind of premeditated or planned decision not to use this valuable means of communication.

Another researcher (Burchett 1967) examined the factors affecting nurse-patient communication in geriatrics, in terms of the relationship between the amount of physical care needed by patients and the amount or type of communication which they were most in need of when receiving this care. She showed, for example, that a seriously ill patient may be too exhausted to cope with anything more than the kind of communication which is vital for his physical care. In these circumstances, the effectiveness of a nurse's non-verbal communication with the patient becomes of paramount importance.

Verbal communication One researcher (Wells, 1980) looked closely at the verbal content of conversations between nurses and geriatric patients. Wells tape-recorded the interactions between nurses and patients on a geriatric ward, and analysed the content of what was said in these interchanges according to three categories: 'procedural', 'personal' and mixed 'procedural/personal'. Her procedural interactions were mainly explanations or directives to the patients about some kind of procedure or task. Personal interactions were those remarks which were concerned mainly with the patient as a person, or with social events inside or outside the hospital. The mixed procedural/personal interchanges combined these two extremes and, indeed, conversations would sometimes begin with a procedural focus, and later develop into more personal communication. The main findings of Wells study are summarised in Table 4.1.

The largest proportion of time spent by nurses talking to patients (75%) was during the giving of physical care, a finding which is in accordance with research by Stockwell (1972) which showed that nurses felt that they had ample opportunity for conversation with patients in the course of their routine delivery of nursing care.

Wells' study did not fully account for the nurses' aims and intentions in communication with patients, although she emphasised that when studying nurse-patient communication it is important to discuss the interactions with the participants in order to discover what were their intentions, purposes and hidden messages. For example, the following conversation took place between a nurse and a patient whilst the nurse was helping this somewhat disorientated patient out of bed and onto a commode. It shows that conversation with a purpose which is superficially 'procedural' may actually have many 'personal' undertones.

N   Edith, you don't look very happy at all, do you?
     You hold my hand.
     Oh, Edith, why are you crying?
     It's too early in the morning. I can't cope with you if you are crying now.

P   I can't.
     I don't know.

N   Oh Edith, what am I going to do with you?
     I'd better get you a paper tissue before it all runs down your face.
     It's a good way of cleaning your face in the morning isn't it?

P   I don't know.

N   It's the tears, I can see it all going down, all through the cracks.
     Give me a big smile, please.
     That's better.
     You've got a tear on the end of your nose.

P   Have you got one (tissue)?

N   Yes I've got tissues, or I used to have.

P   Thank you.

N   All right, just take one. That's it, now a big blow.
     That's made you feel better.

Please say yes, otherwise I'll start crying.
Go on, say yes.

P   Yes.
Thank you.

N   Good.

Wells (1980) p.18

This nurse could be employing (not altogether successfully) a sophisticated 'reflecting' technique* in order to demonstrate her understanding of the patient's feelings and to offer her support. Alternatively, she might be attempting to suggest positive behaviour to a mentally impaired patient. On the other hand the nurse may be experiencing despair and frustration at her own inability to understand the patient's emotional responses, and her comments may reflect this despair. In order to understand the nurse's motivations and intentions in this conversation, it would be necessary to hear what the nurse herself said about them, how she interpreted the patient's behaviour and why she felt it appropriate to respond in that particular manner.

Wells found that entirely personal communication between nurses and patients was infrequent and usually social in nature. Where two nurses were attending to one patient, she found that they often conversed with each other, leaving the patient to assume the position of a third person on the edge of a conversation which might involve them without including them. The average length of sustained verbal conversations was also measured during the course of this research, and was found to be approximately one minute thirty seconds. The brevity of the conversations indicates that the nurses did not give high priority to this aspect of a patient's care.

This work by Wells is important because conversations were recorded 'live' on tape. The nurses and patients in the study adapted quickly to the presence of the researcher with a tape recorder but even if these findings are in any way distorted by the intrusion of the researcher, one would expect a rosier picture to emerge. Certainly, the overwhelming impression from this research is that of infrequent communication between nurses and patients, and communication of a limited and routine kind.

*See, for example, Chapter 6 page 88–89 for an account of this technique.

All these studies established the need for improving both verbal and non-verbal communication skills with elderly patients. This priority has implications for both nursing practice and nursing education, particularly in the light of changing policies in geriatric care.

Changes in geriatric care and their impact on communication

In recent years there has been one major change in geriatric care which, in theory, could have influenced the nature of nurse-patient communication. This is the move from what is often called custodial or institutional care to nursing which emphasises the rehabilitation of the patient, and his return to a self-sufficient life in the community. The emphasis of care has shifted from simple physical care to a more overall consideration of the geriatric patient and his individual and social needs. Undoubtedly, some old people are still being nursed in decaying Victorian buildings with cramped wards and narrow corridors which are neither conducive to close communication between the patient and the nurse, nor to the rehabilitation of the patient. However, an increasing number of geriatric patients are nursed in purpose-built units which reflect some recognition of their needs both for privacy and for sociability. These units include individual bed curtaining and pleasant communal living areas.

It is now more common to see patients sitting in small groups in the dayrooms, where previously they sat lined up against the walls. This kind of change in the physical environment helps to encourage conversation between the patients, and allows friendships to develop and be maintained on the ward. However, during the course of my work I have heard many patients expressing dislike for the dayrooms, and such patients often ask if they may stay in the bed area. This may be because individual patients dislike the enforced sociability which the dayroom involves, but it may also be due to the fact that the nurses rarely appear in the dayroom and consequently patients' opportunities to discuss or communicate with the nurses when they are in the dayroom are very limited.

This shift of emphasis towards increased rehabilitation in geriatric care will undoubtedly result in changes in the role of nurses for geriatric patients. Nurses will not only be required to continue giving necessary physical care but will also be expected to influence and modify the patients' behaviour. For example, this may include nursing regimes such as regular toileting to encourage continence – the management and modification of 'continence behaviour' can obviously benefit both the nurse and the patients. However, geriatric patients now spend most of their day out of bed in the company of other patients. It is important therefore to learn to nurse geriatric patients in chairs, and not only individually but also in groups. Nursing education has yet to come to terms with this change of practice, and hence nurses may fail to respond to these new and challenging developments. The result for the patient may be a day spent in a splendidly furnished dayroom which is seldom visited by nurses.

A further recent development in the care of the elderly, and particularly psycho-geriatric patients, is called reality orientation. This approach was originated by Folsom in 1958, and stresses the need for patients to relearn (if necessary), and then continually use, a range of basic information relating to his orientation in time and place, and as a person (Miller 1977). This technique involves using a patient's name frequently and encouraging him to use his own name and those of his companions in conversation. Conversations with the staff emphasise the day of the week, the time of day and the hospital ward and locality. One of the techniques involves coloured doors and large labels which may be used to help the patient find his way about so that, for example, one of the labels in the ward might read 'Do you want the toilet? Please follow the yellow lines' (Conroy & Clarke 1977). This kind of reality orientation may be carried out formally in classes meeting on a daily or weekly basis, or it can involve all of the staff informally during their continuing contact with the patient. This kind of approach requires cooperation between all the professions charged with caring for geriatric patients, and it holds a great deal of promise for the well-being and rehabilitation of confused and demented patients who are often overwhelmed and enveloped by institutional care.

Factors affecting communication with geriatric patients

As people grow old, their mental and physical faculties can be dulled, or damaged by illness or accident. This can result in temporary or permanent impairment which in turn will affect the patient's ability to communicate. Some of these impairments and some of the strategies and procedures which can be used to overcome each of the resulting barriers to communication are now discussed.

Poor hearing   Hearing impairment is common in the elderly and arises from a variety of causes including otosclerosis, otitis media, mastoiditis and Meniere's disease. Deafness can be an isolating experience to patients who are just beginning to suffer from its effects. And later on, years of not being able to participate in social conversations can lead elderly people to withdraw from any kind of social situation as a matter of course. One student nurse recently commented to me about an old lady who always sat in the corner by the wall with a shawl over her head. This woman had been always deaf and had become used to her solitude, yet during social conversations the nurse was amazed at the woman's ability to converse intelligently, and fascinated by her account of her days as a music teacher. It may require a great deal of effort on the part of a deaf person to organise the sounds which she hears into meaningful language, but it can be equally frustrating and time consuming for the nurses to speak clearly and carefully enough to an old person for her to understand what is being said. There are times when the geriatric patient and the nurse find that they do not possess the necessary energy or motivation to carry out this kind of communication.

Strategies which may improve communication   The most common solution to hearing impairment is to provide the patient with a hearing aid, although this must be fitted and adjusted correctly if the resulting sound is not further to confuse the frail or elderly. Shouting is not the answer; the nurse should speak in a low-pitched voice of normal volume, always directly facing the patient if this is possible. A sensible precaution is to cut down outside noise such as loud television programmes when communicating with patients who have poor hearing.

Poor eyesight   Limitation of vision is also common in the elderly, arising from conditions such as glaucoma, cataracts, myopia or hemianopia. Where eyesight defects are severe, this may result in the old person being fearful both of strangers and of unfamiliar surroundings as well as having restricted mobility. If the condition is of long standing, the old person will know whereabouts his eyesight is clearest/strongest within his overall visual field, and so anyone talking to the patient should take care to ask the patient where she should sit or stand in order that she can best be seen. A patient with glaucoma will see those objects best which are in the centre of his field of vision, a person with cataract, those at the edge; and for the person with hemianopia, those on the unaffected side of the head can be seen most readily.

Strategies which may improve communication Calm, distinct speech does much to reassure a disturbed patient who has limited vision, and it is important for the nurse to remember that she cannot be seen well by the patient. Therefore she should introduce herself adequately, particularly on a ward where a large number of people may come into contact with the patient. Obviously, a patient who needs glasses should have them, and these should be clean enough to have some effect. If patients lose their glasses, or wear them when they are dirty, this can also lead to sensory deprivation and confusion.

Speech difficulties A loss of the ability to express oneself properly through speech or a loss of verbal comprehension is usually termed aphasia. This does not mean that the patient is deaf, although deafness may be an additional problem. This point is not always appreciated by nurses, and people who have experienced aphasia and have subsequently recovered often say something like 'They spoke to each other about me as though I couldn't hear, almost as though I wasn't there. When they did speak to me they shouted to me as though I was stupid.' Aphasia is a common accompaniment of stroke, a condition frequently encountered in geriatric patients. Although aphasia is a source of frustration for both patients and nurses, its degree may vary considerably from patient to patient, and from time to time. Aphasic stroke patients with right-sided paralysis may have hesitant, scant and paraphasic spontaneous speech. Their ability to repeat words and name objects may be more or less impaired, but their comprehension of things spoken to them tends to be very good.

Strategies which may improve communication   It is important for nurses to realise that aphasic patients may often understand far more than they are able to indicate. This means that a great deal of care needs to be taken in conversation with such patients, and non-verbal communication may provide many important clues to what they are thinking. In many patients, sight may be affected at the same time as speech, so that nurses who begin to talk to aphasic patients whilst they are out of their field of vision may startle and agitate them. A nurse talking to an aphasic patient should look directly at him, and enunciate slowly and clearly. Ordinary conversational speech can sound scrambled and unclear to the aphasic patient, with the result that he may utter a stream of meaningless words or even 'perseveration' of a particular obscenity which may alarm staff and relatives.

Christo (1978) emphasises the importance of helping aphasic patients to relax as such patients tend to become tense and frustrated, and this may make their attempts to communicate almost meaningless. Tension can be released by humour or even by relaxation exercises, and in addition, it is obviously important to provide such patients with frequent mouth care and care of their teeth and dentures. Aphasic patients also need plenty of time in order to take in what is being said to them, and to formulate a reply; any sense of rushing will delay communication by confusing and agitating them. In addition, background noise should be minimised if the nurse wishes to engage the patient in conversation. However, outside sources of stimulation such as the television or the radio may aid the patient's recovery if used during solitary periods.

A patient who has suffered a stroke, with consequent aphasia is likely to be poorly motivated, depressed and may make slow progress in overcoming his sensory difficulties. To counteract this, a nurse should relate her conversations to matters which clearly interest the patient, and here some knowledge of his family, friends and circumstances is essential. If speech therapy is instigated, the nurse should try to be involved in the programme, so that she can use her routine conversations with the patient in the most constructive way possible.

Geriatric sufferers from aphasia are a good example of a group of patients who may benefit from using 'non-verbal message boards' which can help the patients and staff to communicate. Most of these

boards consist of letters which enable the patie.
out messages. Some may incorporate pictures o.
drinks, combs, a bed, or the toilet. These can be usea .
nurses to communicate basic needs, although their su
clearly be limited by the patient's physical ability and .
alertness. Hardiman and his co-workers (1979) report the use
these boards in geriatric nursing, and show that severely handicapped old people can be helped to communicate in this way.

Pain   The ways in which patients tolerate and express their pain
depend upon both physiological and cultural factors. For example,
some elderly patients become so used to chronic pain that they
appear to tolerate it remarkably well, whereas acute and intermittent
pain will cause them more visible distress. Communication between
nurses and patients who are in pain requires sensitivity and observation skills on the part of the nurse.

Strategies which may improve communication   A very common
reaction amongst nurses towards patients in pain is to attempt to distract attention from the source of the pain. Unfortunately, this
response can result in the nurse effectively ignoring the patient's distress. Distraction can be a useful strategy if it is used *after* everything
possible has been done to involve the patient in discussions about the
pain and how it affects him and in decisions as to how it can be
managed. Pain-relieving drugs, while often very helpful, can produce
extra symptoms of lethargy, drowsiness and confusion in elderly
patients. There is often a strong association between pain and
anxiety, and this indicates that time should be spent with the patient
who is in pain, since this in itself may enable him to cope. For example, a man whose intolerance of a chronically painful condition
was at a low ebb was heard to ask a student nurse if she would play
chess with him. It was, he felt, the only thing that could take his mind
off the pain.

Fatigue and tiredness   Fatigue is a feature of most illnesses, and is
not unique to geriatric patients. However, it is particularly prevalent
in elderly patients who are adapting to sensory deficits, and also
amongst old people who are constantly required to communicate
with strangers, such as the wide variety of medical and para-medical

aff found in hospitals. In addition, metabolic disturbances such as .nyxodema may produce symptoms of unusual apathy and loss of motivation amongst elderly patients.

Strategies which may improve communication   Nurses frequently observe that patients suffering from fatigue have 'best' and 'worst' times during the day. Old people have different patterns of fatigue to' those of younger adults, and they also take longer to recover from strenuous activities. Therefore, care must be taken in planning the patients' day so that undue stress and fatigue are avoided, and procedures or tiring discussions only take place when the patients are best able to cope.

Confusion   Communicating with disorientated patients is a particular concern of most geriatric nurses. The fact that their concern is not always for the patients' welfare is reflected by the following comments which I gathered from student nurses after they had been working in a geriatric ward for only a few days:

> 'Some of the patients you can't get any sense out of – they don't hear you.'
> 'It was such a relief to find someone who could talk back and you could have a sensible conversation with.'
> 'Some of the patients have only got one conversation, and once you have had it, you've had it.'

A patient may be disorientated in terms of people, places, or time, or alternatively his disorientation may be the result of his failing to understand conversations, so that his contribution will be inappropriate. Disorientated patients also suffer from diminished short-term memory, and they rely upon their longer-term memory as the basis for everyday conversation. For example, many disorientated old people refer to events, values, and relationships which existed several decades ago as if they were 'only yesterday'. The most common causes for such disorders are cerebral haemorrhage, cerebral thrombosis and cerebral arteriosclerosis.

Strategies which may improve communication   Obviously, the nurse communicating with a confused and elderly person must not wander off the point of conversation herself, and she should be prepared to re-emphasise whatever point she is trying to make on several occasions. The reality orientation techniques discussed earlier in the chapter can be particularly useful with disorientated patients, as they provide a means of using objective evidence such as clocks, calendars, signs and colour coding to reorientate the patient in his surroundings.

The nurse's role in communicating with geriatric patients

The quality and quantity of nurse-patient communication in geriatrics is affected by the nurse as well as the patient. The nurse's attitudes, values, and the tasks she is set to perform can all affect the kind of communication which takes place between herself and her elderly patients.

Nurses' attitudes   Some of the attitudes which nurses traditionally hold in respect to geriatric patients can act as a very effective barrier to communication. For example, Davis (1978) suggested that the nurses themselves may be responsible for much of the eccentric, erratic and childish behaviour in elderly patients by virtue of their expectations that all geriatric patients behave this way, and they may in consequence unwittingly socialise the patients to do so. So long as the nurse only pays attention to patients when they scream for attention or when they are noisy, it is hardly surprising that patients learn to behave in this childish manner in order to gain the nurses' attention. A vicious and downward spiral is set in motion.

The nurse's attitudes will influence both the style and content of her communication with the patient. Kogan (1961) showed how positive attitudes towards old people were associated with a 'nurturing' concern for others. A nurse with a positive score on Kogan's attitude scale would probably want to nurture old people with signs of dependency. However, a key question surrounds how far this is desirable, for it seems likely that many elderly people need something more than nurturing care if they are to maintain their independence in line with the current ideology of geriatric medicine which emphasises rehabilitation and independence for the old person. There is obviously no single and ideal balance between nurturing old people and promoting their independence, but it is important that the nurse considers how far her actions, and basic attitudes towards the patients in her care will lead to their becoming more or less dependent upon her.

Close communication between nurses and patients who are both elderly and ill can be very demanding for the nurse. The young student nurse confronted with elderly patients is often dismayed and shocked. The nurse may also feel that her own professional image of 'the nurse', as someone who plays a part in the patient's recovery, is threatened by the elderly and the dying. As a defence against this, the nurse may find it difficult to communicate with the patient as a person, and she may maintain the relationship in a purely functional manner by giving the patient basic physical care rather than sharing in his experience. An important skill for the geriatric nurse to acquire in such situations is listening, since she often has little personal experience to draw upon. However, her willingness to stand alongside a patient who is distressed and anxious may give him something which words cannot express – even the words of an experienced geriatric nurse. In addition, special skills in communication are required when dealing with patients who have particular diagnoses. Burchett (1967) looked at the influence of diagnoses upon communication patterns. She found that, for example, the diagnosis of a chronic brain syndrome or dementia may be as stigmatising as a diagnosis of syphilis and, in consequence, may greatly reduce the willingness of other people (such as fellow patients and nurses) to spend time in contact or conversing with a patient. An important implication of this research relates to the nurses' need for preparation and support in this area of nursing, particularly in terms of the high emotional risk to nurses caring for the elderly and patients nearing death.

Conclusions

Orlando (1961) suggested that the purpose of nursing is to 'supply the help a patient requires in order that his needs may be met'. In the case of geriatric patients, there is a great temptation to categorise the person as a 'patient', and submerge the individual differences between patients. This kind of depersonalisaton makes nurses deal with geriatric patients as objects upon which tasks must be performed (Travelbee 1971).

The importance of talking to patients has been eulogised in all fields of nursing, and yet it is often only given lip service in nursing education; consequently, it has taken a poor second place to procedures and tasks which are taught assiduously in our schools of nursing. One comment is often heard (and not only in geriatric wards): 'If only we had more time to talk to patients'. However, when nurses' work is examined more closely, a large percentage of time seems to be taken up by non-nursing duties and personal time (Wells 1980). The simple fact of life is that, for many nurses, talking to patients is low on their list of priorities, and Stockwell (1972) also showed that neither nurses nor patients feel that talking constitutes an important activity.

However, nursing *is* increasingly being seen in terms of fulfilment of patients' needs rather than the accomplishment of a range of routine nursing tasks. This trend is being increasingly supported by developments such as the nursing process, as well as current changes in the ideology of geriatric medicine which emphasise the patient's independence, individuality, and ultimate potential for rehabilitation. It is to be hoped that these two influences will be beneficial both for geriatric patients, and their nurses.

References

Blazer D. (1978) Techniques for communicating with your elderly patient. *Geriatrics*, Nov., 79-84

Bloom M. Duchon E., Frires G., Hanson H., Hurd G., & South V. (1971) Interviewing the ill aged. *The Gerontologist*, **11**, 292–9

Burchett D. E. (1967) Factors affecting nurse-patient interactions in a geriatric setting. *ANA Regional Clinical Conferences*. New York: Appleton-Century Crofts

Burnside I. M. (1973a) Touching is talking. *American Journal of Nursing*, 2060–2063

Burnside I. M. (ed) (1973b) *Psychosocial Nursing Care of the Aged*. New York: McGraw-Hill

Christo S. A. (1978) Nursing approach to adult aphasia. *Canadian Nurse*, **74** (7), 34–39

Conroy C. & Clarke P. J. (1977) Reality orientation: a basic rehabilitation technique for patients suffering from memory loss and confusion. *Occupational Therapy*, 250–251

Davis R. W. (1968) Psychologic aspects of geriatric nursing. *American Journal of Nursing*, **68**, 802–804

DeWever M. K. (1977) Nursing home patients' perception of nurses' affective touching. *Journal of Psychology*, **96**, 163–179

DHSS (1978) *A Happier Old Age*. London: HMSO

Dominian J. (1971) The psychological significance of touch. *Nursing Times*, **67**, 896–898

Hardiman C. J., Holbrook A. & Hedrick D. L. (1979) Nonverbal communication systems for the severely handicapped geriatric patients. *The Gerontologist*, **19** (1), 96–101

Hood M. (1977) You don't always need words to communicate. *Nursing Care*, **10** (8), 28–29

Johnson B. S. (1965) The meaning of touch in nursing. *Nursing Outlook*, 59–60

Kogan N. (1961) Attitudes toward old people: the development of a scale and an examination of correlates. *Journal of Abnormal and Social Psychology*, **62**, 44-454

McCorkle R. (1974) Effects of touch on seriously ill patients. *Nursing Research*, **23** (2), 125–132

Miller E. The management of dementia: a review of some possibilities. *British Journal of Social and Clinical Psychology*, **16**, 77–83

Orlando I. J. (1961) *The Dynamic Nurse-Patient Relationship*. New York: G.P. Putnam's Sons

Smith P. (1964) Myth and method in nursing practice. *American Journal of Nursing*, **64**, 68

Stockwell F. (1972) *The Unpopular Patient*. London: RCN

Travelbee J. (1971) *Interpersonal Aspects of Nursing*. Philadelphia: F. A. Davis

Wells T. J. (1980) *Problems in Geriatric Nursing Care*. Edinburgh: Churchill Livingstone

Chapter 5: Communicating with Patients and Relatives in Intensive Care Units

The special demands and challenges of communicating with patients in intensive care units are examined in this chapter. Inevitably, such units tend to be the focus of much stress and anxiety which is shared by patients, relatives and nurses. This stress means that although effective communication between nurses, patients and relatives is vital, it can become fraught with problems.

The author examines some of these difficulties and discusses ways in which they can be overcome by drawing upon her own experience and research undertaken in an intensive care unit. One particular and extreme problem often encountered in such units occurs with patients who are on ventilators and paralysed. Such patients are unable to speak or move, and in these circumstances it is essential that nurses should develop accurate observational skills and other skills in non-verbal communication. Once again, the need for these skills to be practised and specifically taught in nurse education is emphasised in this chapter, and this is linked to other developments in nurse education – in particular to the introduction of the nursing process. In this context it is worth reflecting whether the growing use of the nursing process will in itself provide an impetus for increased education in communication skills for nurses.

Pat Ashworth trained as a nurse at Kent County Ophthalmic and Aural Hospital, and at Guy's Hospital, London. She also completed midwifery training and held various posts as a staff nurse and ward sister. She has spent many years working in the field of intensive care, including more than nine years as departmental sister in a 12-bedded ICU. She was awarded an MSc for her research into communication between nurses and patients with endotracheal tubes, and subsequently held a joint appointment as ward sister/lecturer in nursing at the University of Manchester where she currently manages a programme of clinical nursing research.

63

Chapter 5

Communicating with Patients and Relatives in the Intensive Care Unit

Pat Ashworth

Introduction

It has been said that hospitals are places cradled in anxiety, where there may be a cycle of anxiety, uncertainty and lack of communication which appears to affect the well-being of both patients and staff (Revans 1961).

Treatment in intensive care units probably evokes more anxiety than any other field of hospital care, and therefore communication between nurses and patients undergoing intensive care is likely to be as vital as it is difficult.

The patients, who may or may not be conscious, are surrounded by the strange sights and sounds of ventilators, humidifiers, monitors, and other equipment. They are often subject to strange and uncomfortable sensations due to infusion lines or monitoring leads attached to them which can make them feel tied down. In the midst of all this, the patients' ability to communicate may also be directly impaired by, for example, bandages which occlude their eyes.

Nurses communicating with patients in the ICU have to cope with the additional stress which is sometimes caused by anxious relatives, the patient's anxiety (which is compounded by his unfamiliarity with his surroundings and his social isolation), and the nurse's own stress, often resulting from her preoccupation with numerous and complex nursing procedures, and sometimes from lack of knowledge and experience of intensive care.

This chapter looks at these special difficulties which nurses face when communicating with patients in intensive care. It does so by examining what is meant by communication between two people, and how stress affects it. Later sections look at the roles of patients, visitors and nurses in the pattern of communication in the ICU.

Many people believe that the use of the nursing process facilitates communication with all kinds of patients, including those in intensive care. This chapter closes by looking at this proposition, and the patients' communication needs during the different stages of the nursing process.

The elements of nursing communication

Just as deficiencies in nutrition can only be understood by considering the various elements necessary for health, such as protein, fat, carbohydrate and vitamins, so communication difficulties can only be understood by looking at the various components of normal communication, and in particular, speech and non-verbal signals such as touch, facial expression and eye contact. Many patients in intensive care units are deprived of some or all of their normal means of communication, and the nurse must be able to assess what these deficiencies are so that she can compensate for them. To do this she needs to be aware of the existence of a range of different channels of communication, and also be able to use them to the best advantage.

Research into human communication indicates that the information conveyed between one person and another is much greater than the content of the words alone. When two people meet for the first time they immediately begin to form impressions of each other's age, racial origin, personality, mood, life-style and other general characteristics. These impressions are based on a range of features communicated by any human being, such as his general appearance, facial expression, gestures, movements, and posture.

Thus in any interaction a great deal of information is conveyed and received, much of it non-verbally and unconsciously using the channels of sight, hearing, touch and possibly even smell. In addition, *not* smiling, not looking at, or not attempting to communicate with the other person also transmits a range of messages. Depending on the circumstances, ignoring another person may indicate 'I'm busy with other things', 'I'm not interested in you', or even 'I do not regard you as a person with whom it is possible (or appropriate) to communicate'. As Wilmot (1975) says, to be 'disconfirmed' or ignored in this way can be worse than being rejected.

To a considerable extent, a person's view of himself depends upon other people's reactions to him. It is difficult for people in general, and patients in particular to maintain their self-respect, their identity and their sense of worth if they are constantly ignored by others, or treated as incompetent, inanimate or childish.

There are many examples of this happening in the intensive care unit, some described in reports by patients of conversations which went on over and around them. One patient being artificially ventilated remarked 'I didn't want to be identified solely as a medical case study . . . Even with dozens of people scurrying about the relationships could be *impersonal* and in contrast to the cold steel of my respirator I wanted the touch of a warm human hand' (Carlson 1968). Another patient in an intensive care unit became so upset about remarks which she overheard like 'She may make it or she may not, but (the surgeon) will get a brilliant article out of this . . .' that she wrote a note to ask the nurse if they knew she could hear (MacKenzie 1970).

Although both these examples are American, similar things happen in Britain, as testified by the patient who remembered a doctor standing at the foot of his bed and saying 'Well, he's had it hasn't he?' (it did happen), or one who became increasingly desperate as he tried to indicate that his bladder was full, but could not convince the nurse because 'You've got a tube in' (it was blocked).

The relationship between stress and communication

There is a good deal of evidence indicating that psychological stressors may produce physiological effects such as changes in cardiovascular function, electrolyte balance, acid-base balance, blood glucose, corticosteriod and catecholamine levels (Selye 1956; Brod 1971; Porter & Knight 1972). Stressors may also cause psychological reactions such as delusions or hallucinations.

An important factor contributing to patients' levels of stress can be the nursing communication or the lack of it. Furthermore, it is known that the effects of multiple stressors are cumulative (Selye 1956); so severe illness or trauma, lack of sleep, pain, anxiety, sensory deprivation or overload are likely to make a person more susceptible to the effects of inappropriate communication. This obviously has important implications for nurses' communication in the ICU. However, the psychological effects of stress, sometimes known as 'ICU syndrome', may also *cause* poor communication, or at least make good communication more difficult. If the patient is deluded and thinks he is in prison, or tied down with people trying to poison him, then he may be more disturbed by the nurse who tells him to 'Stop pulling at those lines and take these pills', even though she may think it is for his own good.

The patients in intensive care units

A number of small research studies seem to indicate the importance for patients' physical well-being of clear and careful communication in nursing fields similar to intensive care. For example, patients inadequately prepared for transfer from a coronary care unit were found to suffer more cardiac complications after transfer than when better prepared psychologically beforehand. (Klein *et al.* 1968). Similarly, in an anxiety-provoking situation, the presence of a nurse may reduce tachycardia in a patient with myocardial infarction (Sczekalla 1973), and in a study by Mitchell & Mauss (1978), discussions of one apparently unconscious patient's condition by his bedside appeared to be related to rises in intracranial pressure.

Two experimental studies, also small in scale (Lazarus & Hagens 1968; Budd & Brown 1974), indicated that good communication by nurses directed towards better patient orientation reduced the incidence of delirium and psychotic symptoms. Patients who were systematically reorientated in the latter study had significantly fewer complications and went home an average of four days earlier than the control group of patients. Although these studies relate to patients who had undergone cardiac surgery, my personal experience supports the evidence of this psychological-physiological interaction in intensive care nursing generally. Maron *et al.* (1973) conclude that since all the body systems interact, when one or more systems fail it is important to support not only those which have failed but all the other systems as well. In this respect, the patients' psychological system is as important as any of the others.

Despite the established importance of communication with critically ill patients, there are strong indications from both nurse researchers (Chow 1969; Kilgour 1970) and ex-patients that communication and emotional support are very inadequate at times. As might be expected, those who suffer most from lack of, or inappropriate, communication seem to be patients who are unable to talk owing to an endotracheal or tracheostomy tube. Worse still, these patients may be paralysed or suffering from some cerebral dysfunction so that they are unable to use any of their normal means of communication.

My own research into intensive care nursing involved 232 hours of observation of patients with endotracheal or tracheostomy tubes in five units, and it serves to illustrate a number of the points made so far (Ashworth 1980). There was a significant correlation between the amount of intentional communication which the patients were able to initiate, and the amount of communication they received from the nurses. In other words, when there was more communication by patients there was usually more communication by the nurses, and vice versa.

The kinds of communication entered into by the nurse also tended to be much more limited when the patient was apparently unresponsive, being confined mainly to warnings of what the nurse was about to do to the patient. For example, in each of two units in the study, a young man with multiple injuries was curarised on one day, and ventilated but not curarised on the second day. In the case of each of the patients, on the second day not only did the nurse talk to the patient on more occasions, but the range and content of their communication was also greater, including social greetings and information about the patient's conditon, care and surroundings, rather than being almost exclusively things like 'I'm just going to turn you over'. Also, on the second day, touch was used in communication for the first time despite the fact that it seems unlikely that the patients' needs for communication were greater on the second day. Indeed, since it is frightening to be paralysed and in a strange place with unfamiliar people, the patient's needs for communication may well have been greater on the first day.

Human beings usually gather information by seeing, hearing and perhaps touching their environment in order to meet their need to understand it, and exert control when necessary. Therefore, the patient who is unable to open his eyes and see, or cannot reach out to touch, or cannot interpret the sounds he hears will need the nurse to compensate for this by telling him about the things he cannot see, and explaining what is strange to him. Just as nurses are able to compensate for patients' inability to wash themselves, so they should also be able to act as a temporary substitute for, say, the patient's inability to see or hear.

The study also showed that nurses in the intensive care unit rarely introduced themselves or other people, and quite often failed to explain what was happening or the cause of sounds such as the alarm on the ECG monitor. They also tended to forget simple aspects of communication such as telling the patient the time, the day, or the date, despite the fact that research indicates that people need this kind of information to keep themselves orientated.

Patients often demonstrate their need to feel some control over their environment, although staff do not always recognise this. Seligman (1975) suggested that humans, like other animals, become anxious or depressed and inclined to 'give up' if they feel unable to control what happens to them. This need for control was illustrated by one patient who described how distressing he found tracheal suction until he realised that it cleared his chest, and that by letting the catheter go down, and not coughing until it became irresistible he could make it hurt less. He then felt that he had some control over the experience, he watched to see how much was aspirated, and found that it no longer troubled him.

Communicating with visitors to the ICU

Nursing staff and patients' visitors can either be a great source of distress to each other, or a great help (Storlie 1976). Staff and visitors are united in wanting the best for the patient, but they may come into conflict with one another as a result of differing priorities. The husband, wife, relative or close friend knows the patient personally, and is able to predict his emotional reactions to the situation. They also rightly feel that their presence can be of help to the patient (see, for example, Thomson 1974; Robinson 1974). Nurses often concentrate solely on the necessary tasks and procedures and may see the presence of visitors as a nuisance, feeling that it prevents them from getting on with their work. They may also feel hampered by visitors who constantly ask for information and reassurance which may be difficult to give when the patient's prognosis is uncertain.

A study of the grieving spouses of dying hospital patients (Hampe 1975) revealed that they need advice on what to do in order to help their loved one, and they also need the staff to allow them to express their feelings. Findings from this study were used in one ICU to improve the care of visitors (Breu & Dracup 1976). When someone has cared for, say, a husband for many years, it is hard to leave him in the hands of strangers. Feelings of helplessness and frustration are likely to be even greater if the nurses apparently fail to recognise the human and individual needs of the patient as the visitor does, yet the visitor is often afraid to touch or talk to the patient in case it does harm or is 'not allowed'. Visitors often need the nurses' help and 'permission' before they can help the patient by touching him and talking to him as they would normally.

Visitors and relatives often have anxieties of their own, for example, 'Will my husband lose his job because of his illness or disability? . . . What if he dies, or perhaps almost worse, lives but is so brain-damaged that he will never again be the same person I knew and loved?' Sometimes this anxiety is expressed in repeated demands for attention, or even aggression, or as a constant demand for information which the relatives then fail to comprehend. However, at first it is often only the visitors who know the patient as a person, and how he usually copes with difficulties. In many cases, nurses can only learn this from the visitors, or from the patient later on as he recovers, so good communication with visitors is of benefit to all concerned.

The nurses' role in communication in the ICU

Nurses are in close contact with patients in intensive care units for 24 hours a day, and often a single nurse is with one or two patients over the whole of her shift. Therefore it seems that nurses hold the key to improving communication with patients, and it is important to consider why this communication is often deficient. Intensive care nurses are often pressurised by the need to make frequent recordings of vital signs, and undertake other tasks of physical care and treatment. Some nurses lack experience of this type of work, and in the midst of it they may be interrupted by doctors, para-medical staff, technicians, visitors, telephone messages and so on. Many emotional pressures also result from constantly nursing critically ill patients, in particular since their welfare may be very susceptible to the effects of nurses' omissions or mistakes. If the ICU nurse develops a close relationship with her patients and visitors this will be to their benefit, but will make emotional demands on her, especially when patients die.

During my study I interviewed 112 nurses about their views on communication in the intensive care unit (Ashworth 1980). Of these, 17 indicated that what they disliked most was the emotional demands of patients and relatives 'especially if the end result is poor'; and a further 14 were troubled by the lack of social interaction with patients who are unable to talk. Table 3 contains some results of my observational study of nurses' communication patterns in the intensive care unit. During the interviews, the majority of nurses said that they tended to talk to their patients about their family, home and other interests, their condition, and things like the time and date. However, since all these things would have come into categories B or E in Table 5.1, it can be seen that this constituted a small part of the content of the nurses' communication.

Overall, nurses in the study recognised that patients need communication from nurses and others, and some had ideas on what the content of this communication should be. However, despite the fact that two of the units ran recognised intensive care courses (JBCNS Course 100), communication was either not specifically taught, or taught only anecdotally.

Improving nurse/patient communication in the ICU

In order to improve the current picture of communication between nurses and patients in the intensive care unit, changes are needed both in education of intensive care unit staff in general, and in the organisation of nursing care in many units. Teaching nurses about the 'importance' of communication in the intensive care unit is all very well, but the students may learn a great deal more by experiencing, say, loss of sight or hearing for a short period of time (much of this can be brought about simply by using bandages).

Nurses should be taught the particular communication needs and difficulties to be overcome in the intensive care unit including the causes and effects of sensory deprivation syndromes in acute illness (Ashworth 1980). They also need to learn a range of straightforward but important skills of interpersonal communication including the ability to convey a sense of warmth and personal interest by tone of voice, words, touch and other means.

Table 5.1   An analysis of nurse-patient communication in four intensive care units over a period of 4 hours

	Unit A	Unit B	Unit C	Unit D	Unit E	All Units
						Summary of communication in all units
Mean staff 'bits'* per 4 hours	157	134	71	46	131	
Mean patient 'bits' per 4 hours	8	20	19	5	53	
% patient 'bits' which were spontaneous	0%	27%	17%	2%	41%	
A Social superficial	3%	4%	4%	4%	8%	5%
B Social concerned	5%	7%	7%	3%	7%	6%
C Short-term informative	45%	24%	34%	30%	29%	32%
D Questions	11%	18%	29%	10%	33%	21%
E Long-term informative, teaching or orientating	3%	8%	3%	7%	11%	7%
F Request or command	30%	20%	8%	22%	6%	18%
G 'Other'	3%	2%	2%	5%	1%	2%
H 'Reassuring noises'	17%	13%	13%	19%	5%	9%
Verbal interactions, when mutual, face-directed gaze occurred	$\frac{73}{329}=22\%$	$\frac{314}{387}=81\%$	$\frac{128}{174}=74\%$	$\frac{128}{189}=68\%$	$\frac{290}{340}=85\%$	
Times touch used	41	76	15	38	22	
Other total non-verbal interaction	0	3	0	4	3	

*For the purpose of this study, a 'bit' was defined as a sentence or part of a sentence which stands on its own as a unit of communication. For example, 'Hello' alone might be one 'bit', or 'Would you like tea or coffee, or . . . ?', even though the sentence is incomplete. This is not the same 'bit' described in Miller (1978).

Most nurses would agree that the general climate and set of values prevailing in a unit are largely set by senior nurses such as the ward sister. This has a profound effect upon the quality and quantity of communication which all the nurses are encouraged to engage in with the patients. If communication is not regarded as important by the ward sister and nursing officer, then it will probably not be very good. It is also unlikely to improve if it is seen as a nice optional extra to be added when there is time, and if trained staff are ignorant of the fact that:

'There is clearly a positive metabolic effect for the well-motivated, secure, optimistic, happy patient. There is an even more dramatic negative metabolic effect for the discouraged patient who has neither interest nor will to live . . . We can and must do much to tilt this balance in the patient's favour.'

(Harken 1974)

Improved communication in the intensive care unit must be encouraged by changes in the systems of nursing care as well as by developments in the nurses' education and training. What is needed is a system which allows nurses to plan for, and meet, the communication needs of each individual patient. There are many possible approaches to the organisation of nursing care, but in practice the nursing process (Marriner 1979) provides a suitable and increasingly well-known framework within which communication in the intensive care unit may be developed. Many authors now agree that the nursing process is characterised by the following four stages: assessment; planning; implementation and evaluation. Authors and researchers in nursing are increasingly using both the nursing process, and the resulting care plans as a focus for improving nurse/patient communication (one example is Holloway 1979 who writes specifically about the care of critically ill patients).

The remainder of this chapter looks at each of the four stages of the nursing process in terms of their implications for communication in the ICU.

Assessing the patient's needs for communication in the ICU

The immediate assessment of a new patient in the intensive care unit includes checking the patient's ability to see, hear, move, understand

and use all his normal channels of communication, remembering that drugs or cerebral damage may modify both his perception and his interpretation of information from the world around him. However, the nurse should also assess his immediate needs for information, explanation, comfort and human contact. These assessments can be made while dealing with any urgent physical problems. It is usually possible to gather other important information about the patient's social background, daily life-style, and personal interests and characteristics from his visitors and relatives if the patient cannot give this information himself. This in itself also helps the family, who often need to talk to someone about the patient.

All of this information is useful to the nurse, who can plan her care taking into account the patient as an individual by knowing something of his life before admission. It also makes it much easier for the nurse to continue to communicate with the patient even if he is unresponsive. For example, nurses found difficulty in communicating on anything but a routine level with a young man whose head injury had left him almost completely unable to respond. However, once they learnt more about his wife, his young sons, his personality, and even the interest of the whole family in football, they were able to relate to him as a person, and they found talking to him much easier.

Assessment of patients' communication needs should also take into account the potential contribution of visitors. One example of this involved a 17-year-old boy with multiple injuries and acute renal failure who appeared far more relaxed and rested better if his father remained with him, talking very little, but quietly sitting with the patient, holding his hand or smiling when the boy opened his eyes. The nursing care plan therefore included arranging for the father to be present when possible and, in addition, the nurses took care to explain to the father what else he could do to help. Other visitors may have less desirable effects on the patients' well-being, and it may then be necessary to plan to limit their visits in some way.

Whatever the outcome of this assessment of the patients' need for communication, it is important that findings are defined and recorded specifically enough for constructive plans to be based upon them. For example, 'inability to speak or open his eyes – potential social isolation and sensory deprivation syndrome' is more helpful than 'sensory deprivation', since it specifies what is lacking, and helps the nurse to plan to use what abilities remain to compensate. This enables nursing care objectives to be planned in detail.

Planning and implementing the communication aspects of nursing care in the ICU

The nursing care plan which results from the assessment stage of the nursing process should contain both the methods by which the patients' essential communication needs are to be met and the content to be conveyed. The plan should specify the minimum, and if necessary the maximum frequency of essential communication by nurses, as well as plans for encouraging helpful communication by others such as relatives, chaplains and paramedical staff.

For all intensive care unit patients the planned nursing care in the field of communication is likely to include:

1 Orientation to the time, day, date, place, people, environment and procedures   This should include information about the patient's treatment, care progress and how he can help himself. This orientation may be achieved by different means and over different periods of time. For example, a visible clock, a calendar, and a daily newspaper to read may allow the patient to keep himself orientated in time if he can see, particularly if there are also outside windows or an alteration in the day and night lighting in the unit. Otherwise the nurse will need to convey this kind of information in conversation.

2 Communication which maintains the patient's personal identity
This may involve conversation about his normal life, his home, family, interests, preferences and concerns. In addition to this, it is worthwhile to offer the patient as many choices affecting his environment or his care as possible, so that he feels that he can still make decisions and have some control.

3 Specific patient teaching on any aspect of his care should be planned early on   For example, many patients with myocardial infarction can begin to learn about their condition, probable length of stay in the unit, and later rehabilitation quite soon after admission. The way in which this is done will vary according to the individual, his condition, and his reaction towards his illness (for example, whether he copes with illness by means of denial, depression or other reactions).

4 Adopting methods to overcome the patients' sensory deficits
At the most simple level, this involves making sure that the patient has any aids which he usually needs, and that these are effective, for example, clean spectacles, or a hearing aid that is in working order.

In the case of patients who are unable to see due to, say, paralysis, swelling or dressings, it is necessary to give verbal descriptions of their surroundings. This may involve explaining, for example, that the strange noise is the portable X-ray machine approaching; or that the moaning heard is another patient who has just returned from having an operation and is not yet awake; or even that the patient is about to feel the cold metal of the doctor's stethoscope on his chest. If the patient is paralysed, the nurse might also open his eyes from time to time so that he can see who is speaking to him.

5 Comforting patients who are confused or hallucinating   In these circumstances it usually helps to acknowledge and accept the patient's delusions or hallucinations, while stating that one does not see or believe the same thing. This, added to the structured reorientation described above, plus visits from his family will all contribute to a return to normal cerebral functioning.

6 Helping the communication of aphonic (ie. voiceless) patients, such as those who are intubated or have a tracheostomy   These may include pencil and paper techniques or 'magic slate', word indicators, alphabets, or pictures on which the patient can indicate what he wants to say; lip-reading; 'finger-writing'; or even the use of an electronic larynx (Ewing 1975). The aphonic patient can also be helped to communicate using small body movements such as a code, with one wink for 'yes', and two for 'no', or even 'tongue out for yes', since several nurses have commented that tongue movements seem to be some of the first to return as curare effects wear off. Other possibilities include more sophisticated electronic aids involving a small screen or a tape on which letters and words can be produced by using a microswitch.

At first sight it might be thought that plans for communication in the intensive care unit, such as the six points outlined above, would already be put into practice by any trained nurse. However, this is not so, and it seems essential to specify explicitly what is needed for each patient. It may be useful to produce standard care plans for communicating with particular groups of patients in intensive care units, such as those who are admitted to the unit and are able to talk and move but require monitoring, or those who are curarised and ventilated (Mayers 1973). These standard care plans could then be modified and adapted for use by each individual patient. For example, part of such a plan for a curarised, ventilated patient might read rather like Table 5.2.

Evaluation of nursing communication in the ICU

The evaluation of nursing communication is a difficult task in itself, and this is obviously compounded when the patient is partly or totally unresponsive, as is the case with many intensive care patients. However, some evaluations can be made against stated goals, and in addition, changes in such vital signs as pulse rate can sometimes provide some clues.

Care planned to meet other problems and aspects of the patient's physical condition may also relate to communication. For example, passive movements performed to increase the patient's circulation and prevent contractures will also provide him with proprioceptive feedback, and communicate the nurse's care and respect for the patient by the way his body is handled.

One form of evaluation which is possible (although widely ignored) for monitoring nurse-patient communication in the intensive care unit is self-evaluation by the nurses. Unit staff should be encouraged to become more aware of how they are relating to patients, and in general, how the patients are reacting to their communication and contact with the nursing staff.

Conclusion

Much has been said about the nurse's responsibilities to her patients, but she too has communication needs. She needs the input of both specialist knowledge required for this work and more immediate information from other staff, particularly doctors, about medical

Table 5.2   Part of a care plan

Problem	Objective
1 Inability to speak, move or open his eyes; potential social isolation and sensory deprivation syndrome.	Will remain orientated to time, place and people, and will not show signs of psychological disturbance.
2 Potential anxiety about surroundings, and emotional deprivation due to separation from family/friends.	Will be able to communicate (when possible) realistic understanding of surroundings, care etc. Will state feelings of security, and personal interest of others. Vital signs will not show changes indicating anxiety in relation to stimuli.

Plan	Evaluation standards
Describe and explain to him surroundings, equipment and care (simply), and reason for admission, and reason for any unusual noises. Ensure that people in contact with patient are named to him. Talk to him by name about his personal interests, eg. home, family, outside life. Orientate to time at least 4 times per shift, and to day and date at least once on day shift.	When able to communicate patient able to state (or answer questions) correctly as to where he is, time, place, people etc. Shows evidence of attempting to interact normally with others. When asked states that he has not had nightmares/ hallucinations, etc.
Use touch to communicate as well as speech. If possible hold patient's eye open when talking to him at times so that he can see you.	
Encourage visitors to communicate by speech, touch etc despite lack of response. Use radio programmes patient usually enjoys to provide interest, but make them audible and tell him what it is. Do not use just as 'aural wallpaper'.	
Encourage him to communicate whenever possible, eg. answer yes-no questions by tongue out, blink or other signs when not fully curarised.	
Plan as above. Especially encourage visitors to show concern and affection for him as they would normally. Make sure no inappropriate discussion occurs within his hearing.	When able to communicate states realistic acceptance of surroundings and care. Expresses feeling of safety, and does not indicate loneliness or feelings of severe deprivation. (May need to be ascertained by questions in conversation.) No evidence of adverse changes in vital signs relating to environmental stimuli.

aspects of the patient's condition, treatment, possible problems and complications. Equally important is help, constructive feedback, and support from the rest of the staff and her seniors, particularly when things are not going well. Cassem & Hackett (1975) have argued that intensive care staff risk their feelings, their self-esteem, and their self-respect during the course of their work, or they may risk dehumanising their patients and themelves. In this situation, staff need the opportunity to talk through feelings of inadequacy, guilt, frustration, or anger which cannot be expressed to the patients themselves.

Good care of critically ill patients is dependent upon good interdisciplinary teamwork, which in turn is dependent upon good communication. However, the staff cannot fully communicate confidence and care if they themselves are 'too much in need of support to give any' (Michaels 1971).

Critically ill patients need nurses who talk to them about more than medical and nursing procedures. They must also give . . . 'the things patients need that we're so unaware of. The little things – like a smile or a touch on the arm . . . a simple 'hello' in the morning, just a nod to let him know not only that he still exists, but that he's still important – and listen . . . It shows that we not only care *for* him but care *about* him' (this was written by a doctor ex-patient, Viner 1975).

The paralysed, ventilated, sedated patient, unable to see or hear properly or ask questions is totally dependent on a nurse to keep him in touch with the world around him. With the help of his visitors, she can transform a cold, lonely, clinical and frightening environment into one which is at least warm, secure and friendly, albeit uncomfortable. In the final analysis, it is the nurse's job to make the intensive care unit a place where the patient feels that everyone is working *with* him rather than *on* him.

References

Ashworth P. (1980) *Care to Communicate*. RCN Research Series. London: RCN

Breu C. & Dracup K. (1976) Implementing nursing research in a critical care setting. *Journal of Nursing Administration*, Dec., 14–17

Brod J. (1971) Psychological influences on the cardiovascular system. In Hill O. W. (ed) *Modern Trends in Psychosomatic Medicine*. New York: Appleton-Century-Crofts

Budd S. & Brown W. (1974) Effect of a reorientation technique on post-cardiotomy delirium. *Nursing Research*, **23**(4), 341–348

Cassem N. H. & Hackett T. F. (1975) Letters to the editor. *Heart & Lung*, **4**(5), 802–804

Ewing D. M. (1975) Electronic larynx for aphonic patients. *American Journal of Nursing*, **75**(12), 2135–2156

Hampe S. (1975) The needs of the grieving spouse in a hospital setting. *Nursing Research*, **24**(2), 113–120

Harken D. E. (1974) Post-operative care following heart surgery. *Heart & Lung*, **3**(6), 893–902

Holloway N. M. (1979) *Nursing the Critically Ill Adult*. Menlo Pk., Calif.: Adison-Wesley

Lazarus H. R. & Hagens J. H. (1968) Prevention of psychosis following open-heart surgery. *American Journal of Psychiatry*, **124**, 1190–1195

Marriner A. (1979) *The Nursing Process*. St Louis, Mo.: C. V. Mosby

Maslow A. H. (1954) *Motivation and Personality*. New York: Harper & Row

Mayers M. G. (1978) *A Systematic Approach to the Nursing Care Plan*. New York: Appleton-Century-Crofts

Michaels D. R. (1971) Too much in need of support to give any. *American Journal of Nursing*, **71**(10), 1932–1935

Miller G. A. (1970) *The Psychology of Communication*. Harmondsworth: Pelican Books

Mitchell P. H. & Mauss N. K. (1978) Relationship of nurse-patient activity to intracranial pressure variations. A pilot study. *Nursing Research*, **27**(1), 4–10

Porter R. & Knight J. (eds) (1972) *Physiology, Emotion and Psychosomatic Illness*. Amsterdam: Ciba Foundation/Associated Science Publishers

Revans R. W. (1964) *Standards for Morale. Cause and Effect in Hospitals*. Nuffield Provincial Hospitals Trust/Oxford University Press

Robinson L. (1974) The patient in an intensive care unit. In *Liason Nursing – A Psychological Approach to Patient Care*. Philadelphia: F. A. Davies

Sczekalla R. M. (1973) Stress reactions of coronary care unit patients to resuscitation procedures on other patients. *Nursing Research*, **22**(1), 65–69

Seligman L. C. P. (1975) *Helplessness. On Depression, Development and Death*. San Francisco: Freeman

Seyle H. (1956) *The Stress of Life*. New York: McGraw-Hill

Storlie F. (1976) The family: thirteen years of observation. *Supervisor Nurse*, Feb., 10–14

Thomson L. R. (1973) Sensory deprivation – a personal experience. *American Journal of Nursing.* **73**(2), 266–268

Viner E. (1975) In Chaney P. (ed) 'Ordeal.' *Nursing,* **5**(6), 27–40

Wilmot W. W. (1975) *Dyadic Communication – A Transactional Perspective.* London: Addison-Wesley

Chapter 6: Communicating with Psychiatric Patients

Forming relationships and communicating with patients is often claimed to be one of the special skills of the psychiatric nurse. Indeed, psychiatric nurses are often given special responsibilities for the development of trusting relationships with patients, and these can only be brought about by close and mutual communication. The author of this chapter outlines many of the communication skills and techniques which have been found useful in psychiatric nursing. She also suggests that some of these psychiatric nursing skills, if used appropriately, could help all nurses to care for their patients. In this connection, it is important to remember that patients in general hospitals also have psychiatric problems, and readers will find Isabel Speight's examples taken from her own experience particularly helpful in dealing with such patients.

This chapter contrasts strongly with, say, Chapter 2 where the emphasis in communication was on giving information and explanations to patients. Here, the skills and tactics in communication are those which enable nurses to increase their rapport with patients – skills such as listening, questioning and encouraging. We hope that this chapter will be read by all nurses, because skills such as these are clearly essential, not only for the care of psychiatric patients, but for the care of all patients and relatives.

Isabel Speight trained as a psychiatric nurse at The Retreat, York, during her career as Nursing Officer and, later, Tutor in the Army Nursing Service. Following her psychiatric nurse training she became interested in developing and using the communication skills she describes in this chapter in non-directive counselling for her students, patients and others. She has continued this work on a voluntary basis throughout her subsequent career as Inspector, and

83

later as Senior Inspector, for the General Nursing Council for England and Wales, and now as one of the Professional Officers of the Joint Board of Clinical Nursing Studies.

Chapter 6

Communicating with Psychiatric Patients

Isabel Speight

Communicating with patients is the essence of psychiatric nursing today, although this contrasts strongly with traditional and custodial views of the work of the psychiatric nurse. Well-managed and sensitive communication by nurses is vital for psychiatric patients' well-being, whether they are in need of care through counselling, or social or psychotherapeutic procedures. This chapter's first focus is upon the way in which nurses working in psychiatry can develop and use interpersonal skills during nurse-patient interactions. It describes how the psychotherapeutic or counselling skills of the nurse are used in individual and group interactions, and suggests ways in which some of the special problems and needs of mentally ill patients can be identified and met by psychiatric nurses using certain straightforward verbal and non-verbal communication skills.

Many nurses caring for patients in other clinical specialities are recognising that they also need some of the communication skills which psychiatric nurses are developing and using if they are to help their patients to accept and cope with their illness, disability or impending death. In my view, these skills are one of the most important things that psychiatric nurses have to offer the general nurse.

There can be few areas of health care more debated and debatable than the role of the psychiatric nurse. An advisory committee which looked at this subject came to the conclusion that:

> '... psychiatric nurses spend much time listening to and counselling patients, that some have an active psychotherapeutic role and all carry out supportive psychotherapy to some degree.' (HMSO 1968).

The editor of the Nursing Mirror (1968) commented on the accuracy of this report:

> '. . . as a thesis on how psychiatric nursing should be conducted in the future, it is a masterpiece. As a truthful report of the present situation in many of our psychiatric hospitals, it is a travesty.'

These two quotations show that there is a great deal of disagreement about the current role of the psychiatric nurse, although the small amount of research literature available on psychiatric nursing should give some indication of the real state of affairs. The relationship between the frequency and duration of one-to-one interaction between nurse and patient, and the formation of a relationship was examined by Altschul (1972). Cormack (1976) calculated from Altschul's data that '. . . approximately 8% of the culmulative time for which nurses were observed were spent in one-to-one nurse-patient interaction, leaving 92% spent on non-interaction activities'. This underlines the pertinence of the editorial comment quoted above.

It may be that a more accurate description of psychiatric nursing today is that given by Dietrich (1978) who states that 'Our day-to-day working definition of psychiatric nursing is that it consists of a combination of procedural, therapeutic and custodial skills which nurses perform in relation to their patients'.

Rapport and empathy

It seems to me that helping psychiatric nurses to develop effective communication with patients has long been ignored because few trained staff know how to teach it, and not all recognise its importance. Both Altschul (1973) and Irving (1978) stress that improving communication involves establishing 'rapport' with the patient, which is defined by Irving as 'the harmonious feeling experienced by two people who hold one another in mutual respect, acceptance and understanding'. This definition, which is one of many, implies that the nurse and patient have achieved at least a social relationship where each has got to know the other. The nurse gets to know the patient in both conversation and in joint activities. The more experience the nurse has in common with the patient, the easier she will find it to talk to him. At this first stage of establishing rapport, the aim of talking to the patient is not to find out about his illness, but to get to know him as a person. Anything that interests the patient is a good starting point, for example, his job, his hobbies, his family, or a recent holiday. While the nurse tries to find out as much as she can about the patient in order to help him, the patient in turn tries to find out as much as he can about the nurse in order to establish whether he can trust her. This kind of 'mutual exploration' establishes the basis for a continuing rapport between the nurse and the patient, and the setting in which a therapeutic relationship can develop.

Like rapport, empathy is a term frequently used in psychiatric nursing, not always knowledgeably. It is worth reiterating that empathy has been defined by Kalisch (1971) and others as 'the ability to perceive accurately the feelings of another person and to communicate this understanding to him'. Cheetham (1977) considers that empathy is an essential element in interpersonal communication and involves 'borrowing' the patient's feelings, although the nurse must remain aware of her own separateness (unlike 'sympathy' in which feelings and reactions are shared). How far this is possible does depend on the nurse's ability to experience the emotions the patient is expressing, at a depth which does not overwhelm her. She must control her response so that the patient does not feel that he must protect her from his own distress. It is quite common for the nurse to be unable fully to 'borrow' the patient's feelings, and then she can go no further than to understand the patient and his experiences. By doing this, the nurse is able at least to appreciate his emotions and view the situation from an external standpoint, and this too can be helpful to the patient.

Talking to patients

Communication is not something 'done' to a patient, but something which nurses and patients share. During their training most psychiatric nurses see many examples of ways in which they can talk to patients, for example, to inform, cajole, persuade or direct them. The purpose of such communication might be getting the patient to do something, such as take his medication, go to occupational therapy or carry out some other task. In these interactions the nurse is really communicating to the patient that she (or the doctor) knows 'what is best' for the patient. However, I have found it useful to keep in mind the five objectives suggested by Burr & Budge (1976) when talking to psychiatric patients. These are:

1 to create a relationship of trust and confidence between you;
2 to help the patient put his problems into words;
3 to draw him back from his world of fantasy;
4 to reassure him and to relieve tension; and
5 to help patients to talk to other people and make normal contacts.

As has already been said, the first of these involves using the communication skills which are implicit in creating any relationship based on empathy. This involves the nurse showing by her remarks and statements that she has listened to what the patient has said, understands what he means, is holding in her mind all the information he has given her concerning his personal life, and that she is concerned to understand his present difficulty and to help him if she can. By using sensitively certain simple communication techniques, the nurse can help the patient not only to put his problems into words, but also to explore them. This should not be done by giving a quick 'easy solution' which tends to result in the patient feeling that the nurse considers his problem insignificant and not worth her concern, but rather by the judicious use of particular communication techniques. There are many possible communication techniques or 'tactics' which can be used to develop and improve communication between patients and nurses. The sections which follow describe a range of the most useful and applicable of these tactics.

1 Reflection   Many psychiatric patients, at some time, make a statement to a nurse something like:

Patient: 'You know nurse, I shouldn't be here.'
      An easy response to this would be for the nurse to say:
Nurse: 'Oh yes you should. You wouldn't be here if doctor didn't think you were ill.'

Few patients would persist in their effort to communicate their real problem after such a response. If the nurse wanted to help the patient explore his problem, of which this statement may not be a true expression, she might respond by using a simple communication technique known as *reflection*. This involves repeating the last part of the patient's statement as a question, for example:

Nurse: 'Shouldn't be here?'

If the nurse decides to use reflection, it is important that she gives the patient her whole attention. She can indicate this to the patient by non-verbal means such as looking at him in a sustained way, by sitting facing him if possible, and leaning forward; and by ignoring any distractions or other demands on her attention. The patient may then respond:

Patient: 'No. I shouldn't be here. I'm not mad.'
     Again the nurse may respond 'Mad?'
Patient: 'No. I don't behave like the other patients. I don't ...'

The response of the nurse to this statement may be to confirm that he does not behave like that, if it is true, and then respond by saying:

Nurse: 'Why do you think you're here?'

I have found it unwise to reflect statements back to patients persistently. Patients tend to recognise the technique after three or four repetitions and understandably, they are likely to resent it. However, it is a useful way to help a patient continue exploring his problem. It is a skill which the nurse can acquire with practice without harming the patient or, for that matter, herself.

2 Recall and feedback   Another technique involves the nurse recalling for the patient any relevant information which he has given to her, perhaps by saying:

Nurse: 'Do you remember when you first came into this hospital you told the doctor that you couldn't manage some problems in your life and this made you feel ...'
     'How do you feel about them now?'

This 'feedback' technique is best practised in simulated situations such as role play by groups of nurses as it can be potentially threatening or damaging to the patient. In this example she is using his past feelings to prompt a response about his 'here and now' feelings. This is intended to help him towards a deeper exploration of his present feelings and not his past behaviour. I have never found it helpful deliberately to recall a patient's disturbed behaviour. To do so can lead to the patient withdrawing from the interaction, or completely and permanently rejecting the nurse. It should be said here that any technique of communication must be selected and used for the patient's benefit and not for the sake of the nurse or, worse still, 'the system.'

Once the nurse has practised and become skilled in some of the many verbal and non-verbal ways of encouraging patients to talk about their problems, she will inevitably experience occasions when she knows she cannot give any further help. At first it is difficult for the nurse to accept her own limitations and even more difficult to admit to them. But because the patient needs further help which she cannot give, it is important for her to be able to say something like:

Nurse: 'I don't think I can help you any further at this stage, but if you agree, I'd like to tell X about this part of your problem because I feel that he can help you.'

3 Closure   Drawing nurse-patient conversations to a close without the patient feeling that the nurse has suddenly remembered she has more pressing things to do is very important. One way I have found valuable is simply to thank the patient for sharing his problem with me and, if this has resulted in the re-experiencing of some painful emotions or experiences, it helps to acknowledge it. Usually it is sufficient to say for example:

Nurse: 'I know how difficult it must have been for you to tell me this. Thank you for explaining it to me, you have helped me to understand your problem and I have learnt from this, too.'

Both trust and confidentiality must be maintained, particularly when the talk gets as deep as this. Yet the nurse may be convinced that it will help other members of the caring team in their work with the patient if they know the content of such a conversation. One way to resolve this dilemma is to suggest that patient tells them himself, or gives the nurse permission to tell them if he feels he cannot do so. Occasionally, the nurse will be certain she must pass on crucial information to other staff, for example, in order to preserve the patient's life even if the patient opposes it. On the one occasion I have done this, I first told the patient that I must do so, and why. Although he bitterly resented it at the time he did not reject my help on future occasions as I had expected him to do.

After this kind of conversation, the patient will often say that he has been helped by talking about his problems. Almost as often he does not say so. The nurse should resist the temptation to ask if she has helped, as any attempt to obtain direct evidence about her own skill may lead the patient to think that she is wanting him to be grateful. Such 'positive feedback' to nurses may come rarely, indirectly, or circumstantially. It is worth remembering that a patient who has shared very real problems with a nurse may feel shame or self-disgust, and find it difficult to treat her normally afterwards. It is part of her skill to avoid this happening, and to help the patient feel comfortable in her presence again.

4 Open questions and summaries When reflection or recall are inappropriate, another way of encouraging patients to talk about things that really matter is to ask 'open questions'. These prompt the patient to continue exploring his own problems once he has begun to do so. Kagan (1975) has developed and formalised this technique. He found, as I have, that open questions help the patient continue to talk without feeling that the nurse is probing into areas he is not yet ready to share, and as in reflecting, the patient has some control over the depth of his self-exploration. Examples of open questions include:

What did you do next?
How did you feel about it then?
What did you say?
What did you really want to say?
Can you say what it was you were afraid would happen?
What actually happened?
What do you feel about it now?

Throughout interactions of this kind it is helpful both to the patient and the nurse if the nurse checks that she has understood correctly what has been said so far. I have found it useful to check my understanding of a conversation simply by saying:

'Now let me make sure I have got this clear so far. I think we have been saying ...'

It is equally helpful if either the patient or the nurse summarises from time to time how far they have got in the interaction. It is normally sufficient to say:

'I feel it might be helpful to us both if we stop for a moment and try to summarise how far we have got. Would you like to do that or shall I?'

At any point in this kind of interaction the patient or the nurse can stop without difficulty. In fact, until I had gained considerable experience in helping patients to talk about their problems using this approach, I found it difficult to maintain my own concentration for longer than twenty minutes in these circumstances.

5 Listening   I have provided a number of examples of the way in which tactics such as reflection and open questions can help the process of problem exploration by the patient himself. An equally effective communication skill is that of listening without commenting or questioning. This requires the nurse to wait out the silences which occur, and allow the patient to use the pauses without any prompting beyond the nurse communicating her concentration, interest and concern non-verbally as has already been described. This is not an easy skill to acquire, and many nurses find it particularly difficult to tolerate silence. Allowing for silence indicates to the patient that the nurse expects him to speak, to take the initiative, and to communicate what is most pressing. It can also underline that there is time for the patient to think or plan what to say next. Listening attentively places great emphasis on non-verbal communication skills, as much can be conveyed during these silences, and the nurse needs to be aware of what she is herself communicating, as well as what she is hearing. It is very easy to show momentary loss of concentration or interest, and this can be interpreted as indifference towards the patient and his problems.

There are times when the nurse realises that a patient's problems or emotions have become too big for her to handle alone, and she needs to call other staff or other patients to that patient's aid. But there will be other times when she is really able to discover the patient's hopes and wishes concerning his illness, his treatment or his nursing care. On the basis of this the nurse can make accurate guesses about her patient's feelings, emotional states, and nursing needs. It is at this point that the nurse may turn from simply enquiring to more active roles such as helping, counselling, supporting or prescribing.

Counselling

The counselling role of the psychiatric nurse is a key one in her general approach to the nursing care she offers patients, whatever their illness or stage of recovery. It is one in which communication is vital. A working party held under the auspices of the RCN Institute of Advanced Nursing Education (1978) examined five definitions of counselling before writing their own definition. I find this definition useful as it underlines the importance of communication in counselling:

> 'Counselling is a process through which one person helps another by purposeful conversation in an understanding atmosphere. It seeks to establish a helping relationship in which the one counselled can express his thoughts and feelings in such a way as to clarify his own situation, come to terms with some new experiences, see his difficulty more objectively and so face his problem with less anxiety and tension. Its basic purpose is to assist the individual to make his own decision from among the choices available to him.'

Verbal communication skills such as those I have mentioned like reflecting, asking open questions and summarising, along with non-verbal skills like attentive listening and empathy, help the patient to express his thoughts and feelings, identify his problems and view them more objectively. To preserve the autonomy of the patient it is right that he should make his own decisions, but sometimes it is necessary for the nurse to suggest the next step in solving his problems.

In my experience, most patients find that writing down their problems, and then placing them in the order in which they feel they want to deal with them makes the problems seem less overwhelming and reduces then to manageable proportions. I have often suggested this as a possible way of making progress. The patient may then agree to the idea of ignoring all but the first on his list, and should be able to start working to resolve it. Sheahan (1979) remarks that, even though it is sometimes necessary to suggest a line of action to a patient, at first he may react to it by rejection, later adopting it as if it were his own idea. He goes on to say that there are times when persuasion may have to be used. However, it is important to emphasise that persuasion depends on the presentation of sound and logical reasons for carrying out a particular action. It is also worth bearing in mind that ready-made solutions often have ethical implications for both the patient and for the nurse herself.

Communication in therapeutic groups

Most of the communication techniques which I have described so far for one-to-one communication are equally effective when used in therapeutic group meetings. Therapeutic communities were developed when it was recognised that social interaction can be used as a means by which patients could help each other and play a critical part in each others' treatment and recovery (Walton 1971). Therapeutic communities are well known for having many group meetings, but group techniques are used in many psychiatric wards (Dietrich 1976). One means of meeting the objective of helping patients to talk to other people and make normal contacts is to involve them in such group meetings. In a therapeutic group the patient encounters new people, and is required to adopt new roles such as the 'enquirer', 'leader', or 'counsellor', and he generally needs to sustain friendly and co-operative behaviour with the other people in the group (Argyle 1972). Nurses find that communication in groups differs in many ways from one-to-one nurse-patient communication as the patients cannot help but relate to each other; the nurse normally adopting a communication style which supports the patients and helps them to talk. As the final goal is usually the social integration of the individual group members, the nurse's main activity is to guide the group in order to make the relationships and activities purposeful and genuine. Dietrich (1976), discussing the purpose of running groups writes:

'Patients who have stopped talking with others in a mutually satisfying manner may in their groups experience a variety of styles of contacting people. They may find ways of resuming their old relationships and of building new ones. This in turn means that there is a greater chance that they may in time restart their lives independent of institutional support. Moreover, an institutional environment which takes account of its patients' presence and holds its patients responsible for contributing to its functioning is comparable to everyday life, because like everyday life it causes interpersonal stresses; withdrawal is more difficult to maintain in the face of others' concern and comments, as are other conventional ways of expressing madness, eg. incoherence, messiness, posturing, etc.'

However, not everything said during a group meeting will be useful even when all the members have agreed the purpose of the meeting. Destructive feelings are sometimes expressed; one particular member of the group may be verbally attacked; or personal questions may be asked of the nurses and other staff present. Altschul (1973) noted that it is not always necessary to answer such direct questions since they can sometimes be deflected by indicating that the staff member is more interested in talking about the patient than about herself. I have found it equally effective just to remind the questioner of the objectives of the group. At other times, it helps the group to continue with their own explorations if the nurse gives a factual answer to the question and then reminds the group that they are straying from their purpose. Alternatively, she might pose a different but related question for the group to consider. I have found that it is not helpful to the group process to respond on an emotional level, perhaps because I find I have to justify my feelings, and this can result in unproductive talk. To questions such as 'Doesn't that make you feel angry?' I have found it best to answer with another question like 'Does it make you feel angry?' and follow the answer with an exploratory question such as 'What makes you feel so angry about it?' It may help the group process to make the subject general to the group by asking questions such as 'Does anyone else feel angry about this?' or 'What is it that makes us feel so angry about it?'

At first it is difficult for a nurse to resist the temptation to respond defensively to verbal attacks on herself or one of the patients in the group. I have found that even the most disturbed patients in a group are able to manage such an onslaught although, occasionally, I have had to intervene by, for example suggesting such an attack was 'not fair'. 'Fairness' is a concept that most young children have grasped, and can be brought home to most of the people in a group of patients.

Where group therapy is in use, or where ward meetings are held, these are usually followed by a staff meeting during which the staff recall and review each interaction of significance and discuss any anxieties concerning their relationships with their patients arising from the preceding meeting. In this way the nurse obtains both information about her performance, and alternative and possibly better ways of responding to similar situations in the future. This review can increase the nurse's repertoire of group skills and responses.

Communication and reality

Psychiatric illness involves a disruption in the patient's ability to relate successfully with others. He may not be able to respond to the nurse who is attempting to talk to him because his 'imaginary' world has temporarily replaced the 'real' one. He still knows what is said and how it is said, and he may respond appropriately by, for example, taking the proffered hand, obeying a request to do something such as sitting down, beginning to eat his meal, or getting ready for bed. It becomes the nurse's task to help him to come even further into the 'real' world. It is important to remember that what the patient sees, hears and thinks is real to him, and proving him wrong or denying his hallucinations or delusions does not help him, indeed it may further alienate him from 'reality'. An example from my own experience may clarify this point.

> When I was walking in the hospital grounds with a patient, who had served in the Army, he said 'If we take this turning we can go and have a meal at the best restaurant in Hong Kong'. I suggested that we sat down on a nearby seat and smoked a cigarette. I remarked how pleasant it was to be sitting in the sun surrounded by such a pleasant garden. He agreed with me and this helped us to talk about the roses we could see and, when asked, he pointed out some roses which he had planted in his own garden. As we stood up I remarked that it was good to be in an English garden on a day like this. He agreed, and as we walked back to the ward our conversation showed that he was, once more, in touch with reality.

Other delusions arise out of inexplicable bodily sensations which patients experience as part of certain illnesses. For example, some patients who are suffering from profound depression can interpret sensations arising from severe constipation, as their body being 'filled with cement' or 'not existing at all'. On the other hand, the young schizophrenic may be certain that he is 'undergoing a sex change'. Assuring the patient that these sensations are part of his illness and that, as he gets better, they will diminish helps him not only to share his anxieties with the nurse, but also to understand their cause and co-operate in his treatment.

Conclusions

As a nurse educator, I tend to emphasise the part played by teaching and learning in the improvement of patient care. However, it is my impression that few tutors attempt to teach their learners communication skills even though they are fundamental to psychiatric nursing care. Cormack (1976) found that there was much evidence to suggest that psychiatric nurse training prepared the nurse mainly for monitoring patient progress rather than for taking an active psychotherapeutic or counselling role. He concluded that more attention should be paid to what are the 'essential ingredients of a caring relationship'. These 'essential ingredients' are debatable but, whatever they are, I am certain that they involve communication skills of a high order.

In this chapter I have outlined the use of verbal and non-verbal communication techniques such as reflecting, using open questions, relating sensitively to the patient, checking understanding and listening as ways in which nurses can help patients to talk about their problems. There are many other simple techniques and approaches which can be used to make conversations (or silences) more purposeful, meaningful, and empathetic. Nurses and their teachers, not just in psychiatry, should be studying and practising this field of human behaviour since it is an essential aspect of their professional expertise, and the care which they have to offer their patients.

References

Altschul A. T. (1972) *Patient/Nurse Interaction: a Study of Interaction with Patients in Acute Psychiatric Wards.* Edinburgh and London: Churchill Livingstone

Altschul A. T. (1973) *Psychiatric Nursing.* London: Bailliere Tindall

Argyle M. (1972) *The Psychology of Interpersonal Behaviour.* Harmondsworth: Penguin Books

Burr J. & Budge U. V. (1976) *Nursing The Psychiatric Patient.* London: Bailliere Tindall

Cheetham V. (1977) *Unpublished Paper.* University of Manchester Department of Nursing.

Cormack D. (1976) *Psychiatric Nursing Observed.* London: RCN

Dietrich G. (1976) Nurses in the therapeutic community. *Journal of Advanced Nursing,* **1**, 139–154

Dietrich G. (1978) Teaching psychiatric nursing in the classroom. *Journal of Advanced Nursing*, **3**, 525–534

Irving S. (1978) *Basic Psychiatric Nursing*. Philadelphia: W. B. Saunders

Kagan N. (1975) Influencing human interaction – eleven years with IPR. *The Canadian Counsellor*, **9**, 74–79

Kalisch B. J. (1971) Strategies for developing nurses' empathy. *Nursing Outlook*, **19** (11), 714–718

Ministry of Health Report (1968) *Psychiatric Nursing Today and Tomorrow*. London: HMSO

Nursing Mirror Editorial (1968) *Nursing Mirror*, **127** (23), 7

Royal College of Nursing (1978) *Counselling in Nursing. The report of a working party held under the auspices of the RCN Institute of Advanced Nursing Education*. London: RCN

Sheahan J. (1979) Mental distress at work. *Nursing Mirror*, **148** (4), 16–19

Walton H. (ed), Jones M., McPherson F. Stock Whittaker D., Sutherland J. D., Walton H. & Wolff H. (1971) *Small Group Psychotherapy*. Harmondsworth: Penguin Books

Chapter 7: Communicating with Patients in Their Own Homes

So far, the contributors to this book have concentrated upon nursing in hospitals. In this chapter the focus turns to the care of patients at home. Nursing care is rather different in the community. Indeed, when the patient is on his own ground the relationship between nurse and patient is also different, and sometimes particularly difficult. This difference in what might be termed the social context within which communication takes place therefore forms the basis of the chapter.

The author has taken an essentially sociological perspective of community nursing care. In doing so she relates the way in which district nurses communicate with their patients to the role they take on when they are in the patients' home. She also examines the tactics which nurses use to encourage patients to co-operate with them, and the tactics which patients use in return. The chapter also looks at ways in which community nurses cope with the possibility of becoming over-involved with patients and their families, and the ways in which they try to help relatives to cope with ill patients at home.

The theme of 'tactics' in nurse-patient communication was introduced by Isabel Speight in the previous chapter, where the tactics involved very detailed aspects of nursing communication such as questioning and listening techniques. However, in this chapter the emphasis is on much broader tactics for encouraging co-operation and compliance, and the author deliberately avoids offering guidelines, hints or prescriptions for practice. Instead, the intention is to encourage readers to think about some important issues related to communicating with patients — for example, involvement with patients and relatives, nurses' roles, and the degree to which nurses can be dominant in all aspects of their relationship with the patients. Although these issues are seen in the context of district nursing in this chapter, they are relevant to every area of nursing.

Jean McIntosh undertook her SRN training at University College Hospital, London. After working as a staff nurse on gynaecological and ENT wards, she did Part 1 Midwifery and then took a BSc degree in sociology. She spent several years carrying out an observational study of district nurses in Scotland and was awarded her doctorate for research into the work of the district nurse.

Chapter 7

Communicating with Patients in Their Own Homes

Jean McIntosh

Introduction

District nurses enjoy a unique relationship with their patients. Their work is largely in the patients' homes, and they have a good deal of autonomy over their nursing activities. They have their own caseload of patients and in consequence, where care is prolonged, their relationships with patients are more enduring than those occurring in hospital. Therefore, the contact and communication that district nurses have with their patients differs in several important respects from the contact and communication which occurs between hospital nurses and their patients.

Firstly, the patients are on their 'own ground', so whereas a ward nurse is more like a 'hostess' who dictates the daily routine, a district nurse is the 'guest' in the patient's home, and has to observe certain rules of guest behaviour. Secondly, in district nursing, patients often relate to one nurse instead of several. The nurses also generally spend longer periods of time in private face-to-face communication with their patients than they would in hospital, and they can expect fewer interruptions. Therefore, communication in district nursing is distinctive and potentially demanding in terms of the relationships that develop between nurse and patient.

This chapter focuses exclusively on communication between district nurses and their patients. It explores the position of the district nurse as a guest in the house, and examines how this can affect communication. Special attention is given to the communication 'tactics' which are used by both nurse and patient. Some of the special problems of nurse-patient communication which may be encountered in the community are also discussed in the light of recent research findings. However, no attempt is made to prescribe rigid rules about how district nurses should best communicate with their patients. The emphasis lies on understanding the complexities of the nurse-patient relationship in this situation, and how these can affect communication.

While there is a certain amount of research which examines aspects of communication between doctors, nurses and patients (well-known examples include Ley & Spelman 1967; Korsch & Negrete 1972; Altschul 1972), almost all of it has concentrated upon hospital settings. The focus of most of the research on communication in the community setting has centred around the extent and nature of the contact between doctors and nurses, eg. Hawthorn (1971). There have been very few research studies which deal exclusively with communication between nurses and patients within the community, although one relevant study has been carried out in the United States by Johnson & Hardin (1962). This research was based on intensive observation of 178 community nurses for one day, and the authors present a list of factors affecting nurses' communication with patients in the community. These factors include the nurses' personal characteristics, for example their marital status, age and educational background; the nurses' attitudes and beliefs about nursing, their aims and goals; the different sorts of home settings in which nurses communicated; and their patients' social and cultural characteristics. A further factor which Johnson & Hardin did not include, but which is arguably as important as the rest, is patients' attitudes and beliefs about their illness, and their expectations of their illness and the care they receive.

It is clear, then, that many complex factors influence what is said between patients and nurses, but few researchers have had the necessary resources of time and money to analyse all of the above factors. For this reason there are gaps in our knowledge and understanding, and it is significant that Johnson & Hardin say that possibly none of the above factors holds the 'real' key to understanding communication between community nurses and their patients. One critical element which they did not examine themselves was the different ways in which nurses actually see themselves, in other words, the roles they see themselves as taking in the home. If nurses take the role of 'hostess' in a ward, and the different role of 'guest' in the home, does this affect the nature of communication in the two settings? Johnson & Hardin suggest that to follow up such an idea might lead to a better understanding of the nature of communication between district nurses and their patients. It was this conclusion that guided my own thinking when embarking upon an observation and time study of 30 district nurses (McIntosh 1975).

A study of communication between patients and district nurses

The primary focus of my study was nursing activities, and so communication was observed in a general, rather than a specific and detailed way. Each of the nurses was observed for a full working week. Discussions of their patients, each nurse's relationships with them, and a variety of problems and conflicts inherent in the community nursing situation, were possible between visits. The observation period for each nurse was concluded by a lengthy, in-depth interview.

A total of 581 visits were analysed for their communication content. This exercise was carried out as a first step along the road towards identifying the range of topics discussed between patient and nurse. A detailed analysis and discussion of the results can be found elsewhere (McIntosh 1979). The main focus of the communication study (based on nearly 2,000 home visits) was an examination of processes at work within the nurse-patient interaction.

Early in the study it became obvious from observation and discussion with the district nurses that the fact that nurses see themselves as guests in their patients' homes determines to a considerable extent the way in which their communication with patients is managed. Having to act as a guest conflicts in many respects with the requirement to act as a professional nurse. For example, a guest does not lay down rules and regulations for her hosts, whereas a nurse often has to do this in the course of her treatment duties.

Many of the nurses I studied mentioned this conflict without any prompting. They explained that they had to learn how to be enough of the 'guest' to enable patients and relatives to maintain the feeling that they were still master or mistress of their own homes, but at the same time exert sufficient influence to establish their authority in respect of the nursing care of the patient. This balance of roles does not always come easily. One nurse remarked: 'At first I went too far, and let the relatives dictate to me – then I thought – I mustn't take what they say at face value. You have to use a little persuasion sometimes.'

As nurses gain experience they learn to recognise that there is no single correct balance between these two roles of guest and nurse. They have to be constantly re-aligned in different situations according to the patients' needs. Consequently, the approach to, and relationship with patients varies widely, as does the amount of nursing intervention achieved, even for patients with the same nursing needs. This constant re-alignment means that sometimes the 'nurse' role predominates, and at other times the 'guest' role is dominant. Some real examples of this conflict illustrate how the process of communication can be affected.

'Guest' in the patient's home

In many homes relatives co-operate in allowing the nurse to determine the way in which nursing care is shared and organised. As the patient's needs increase the community nurse will visit more frequently, and may also call on additional assistance such as a home help or a night nurse. However, a high proportion of the nurses studied had on their caseload a very ill or frail patient whose wife or daughter insisted on undertaking a very large share, if not all, of the nursing care, including night attention.

This situation was clearly demonstrated in a series of visits made by a senior nurse to the home of a man in the terminal stages of cancer. The nurse knew that the wife might not recognise the possible dangers to her own health of an excessive burden of nursing. Her approach to both the patient and his wife was cautious, with an emphasis on tactful questions, rather than advice. She only made suggestions when it was quite clear that to do so would not undermine the wife's feelings of competence. But during the period of observation the nurse became anxious about the wife's state of health. She considered various alternatives, and eventually offered the services of a night nurse to ensure that the wife managed to get some proper sleep. The offer was refused, and the nurse was then left with the problem of whether, and how to exert more pressure on the wife to accept more help. She felt that the only acceptable course of action was to wait until the wife showed further signs of strain, and then to repeat the offer of more help more insistently.

There can be different manifestations of this problem in visits to elderly patients. Not all elderly patients who are referred for care actually see themselves as ill or in need of attention. For some, acceptance of nursing attention may represent an unwelcome decline into permanent dependence. One instance of this involved an old gentleman who had misunderstood that the bath was to be a regular weekly event. On her second visit he greeted his nurse with a determined 'I'm for no more baths'. Once inside the house, the nurse was quick to use the situation to her advantage. She pointed out that everything was ready, and that it could all be accomplished quickly. Still the old man demurred: 'Well you won't be back 'cos I don't care for this racket'. Realising that the outcome of this visit would be crucial for winning co-operation on further visits, the nurse remarked that her main concern was his sore groins, and that she would be satisfied if he allowed her to treat them. The patient acquiesced. So, by drawing his attention to a condition which it was possible to cure, the nurse implied that her visits might be self-limiting, and by this she won his temporary co-operation.

The role of 'guest' becomes more difficult to manage when relatives or patients fail to achieve an acceptable standard of care. It is possible that such relatives try to discourage nursing visits because they resent an intrusion into a routine that they sense is inadequate, but which they are unwilling to change. Such a problem was faced by one nurse caring for a man suffering from hemiplegia following a stroke. She had succeeded in establishing a weekly visit for a bed bath. However, the patient's wife did not welcome her help, and openly showed her resentment. The patient was sadly neglected, his room was dusty and untidy, he was left alone regularly for long periods, and nurse believed that he did not receive any help with washing in between her weekly calls. One or two hints that she made about improving his care had already met with a hostile reaction, so her foothold in the home was tenuous. Accordingly she gave care without offering any advice; she made as few demands on the wife as possible; and was even reluctant to request clean linen. In circumstances such as these, the importance of achieving at least minimal standards of physical care must take precedence over the maintenance of quality nursing care. However, this adoption of a passive guest role is not always appropriate. In certain situations the 'guest' role has to give way to the far more assertive 'nursing' role.

'Nurse' in the patient's home

It is significant that the situations where the 'nurse' role pre-dominated were fewer in number than those where the 'guest' role took precedence. They were, moreover, confined to two main patient problems namely terminal illness, and an inability on the part of relatives to provide adequately for the patient.

Some terminal or very ill patients reject care because they do not wish to be disturbed. In such cases the nursing requirements are so clear-cut that care is seldom withheld. Thus the nurse goes against the patient's wishes, but in the most tactful manner.

This is illustrated by another series of visits which shows how a particular set of circumstances can lead to the 'nurse' role overriding the 'guest' role. A senior nurse was visiting a patient with advanced disseminated sclerosis whose care was shared by her husband and a neighbour. During one visit the nurse noticed that the husband was limping. Her enquiries revealed that he had hurt his back quite severely while lifting his wife. Immediately the nurse said that the patient should be admitted to hospital for two weeks while he recovered. The husband objected strongly, but the nurse remained resolute. He continued to resist, voicing fears that his wife might not be discharged. The nurse reassured him that this would not be the case, and then enlisted the wife's support in persuading him that to continue to care for her would lead to greater discomfort, and perhaps permanent damage to his back. Reluctantly he gave in, and within 24 hours the patient was admitted to hospital.

The second instance where the 'nursing' role is dominant exists in homes where the domestic routine and level of cleanliness are poor, and where, in consequence, the nursing environment is chaotic and dirty. In such situations, all nurses were observed to 'take charge' and adopt an organisational role which sometimes extended to giving advice about the wise use of money, the importance of proper laundering, basic household and personal hygiene, and other subjects which, if raised in other homes, might have caused offence.

It seems, therefore, that opposition to care during serious illness, and a sustained chaotic and dirty nursing environment are two factors which allow nurses to abandon the 'guest' role. As the nurses I observed who dealt with such problems never aroused resentment, they must have been skilled at recognising situations where asserting their nursing role would not threaten their future relationship with the family. This is clearly crucial in situations where the patient's well-being is threatened if the nurse does not insist that the patient and family accept her help and advice.

Tactics which patients use in communicating with nurses

In addition to the problem of balancing the two conflicting roles of 'nurse' and 'guest', district nurses need to be aware of patients' 'tactics' and find a way of dealing with them. The patient tactics which I observed included: trying to get the nurse to spend longer with them; do more for them; see them more frequently; and not discharge them.

One nurse summed up the problem: 'Some of these patients, they're good actors and actresses, you know; you think that they're absolutely helpless, and then the home help whispers to you that they were across the road visiting friends. It's difficult to know how much they do behind your back.' It is sometimes difficult for district nurses to persuade patients that they are ready for discharge.

The following illustration demonstrates patient tactics in such a case:

Shocked at being told that her ulcer had healed, one patient said:

Patient: 'You *really* mean you're not coming back? Are you absolutely sure I'm all right?'

Nurse: (Firmly) 'Yes you're fine. Your ulcer has done very well. Just ring the district nurse if you're worried about it . . .'

Patient: 'Oh but you'll be popping in I expect, one day, to see how I'm doing?'

Nurse: 'Well I have a lot of ill people, and I don't have time to pay social calls. I'll come if you're needing any more attention to the leg. But ring headquarters if you're worried.'

Patient: 'Well please stop for a few minutes if ever you have time.'

Nurse: (Emphatically) 'It's very kind of you, but I'm not promising.'

Outside the nurse explained: 'Some patients do react like that, and you have to be very firm. It's so easy to feel sorry for them but if you weakened you'd be popping in to see half the town'. Therefore, in response to patients' tactics, nurses develop tactics too.

Nurses' tactics in communicating with patients

It is perhaps in caring for old people that nurses develop tactics most consciously as a means of achieving their own goals. In order to win an old person's confidence and gain acceptance of nursing care, nurses may have to adopt a number of different approaches. One nurse's experience illustrates this well. She was caring for an elderly, eccentric lady, and her main task was to organise the old lady's tablet-taking. However, because of the patient's generally unkempt state, the nurse wanted to give her a regular bath. This suggestion offended the old lady deeply, so the nurse had to choose an appropriate tactic whenever the issue was raised. She said 'I always mention a bath, but I vary my approach. Sometimes I ask as if the idea has only just occurred to me. Sometimes I am more determined-sounding. Now and again she gives in'.

There is also another set of tactics which nurses were observed to use in the course of caring for cancer patients. Most of these centred around ways of handling direct questions about the patient's diagnosis. For example one patient said to her nurse: 'It seems I'm going downhill?' This was put in such a way that it could have been either a question or a statement. The nurse commented afterwards that she had felt that the patient was testing her. She explained: 'I usually deny everything. I try to help them accept each stage of worsening as some stage that is to be expected before recovery sets in'.

Another nurse had a more difficult situation to deal with. She visited a male patient suffering from carcinoma of the lung, shortly after he had had a haemoptysis. His wife was distraught, and kept insisting that the blood had come from the throat. The nurse asked appropriate questions at carefully spaced intervals in an attempt to reduce the wife's anxiety, although it seemed that the wife suspected the diagnosis, and was trying desperately to construct an alternative which was less frightening. In this situation, the nurse's tactics and whole demeanour assisted the wife's attempts to delude herself about her husband's state of health. When I discussed the visit with this nurse afterwards, she agreed that she had been deliberately using this kind of diversionary tactic.

The above example emphasises the fact that there is often a vital 'third party' in nurse-patient communication in the community,

namely the patient's relatives. No study of nurse-patient communication in the community is complete without reference to
the nurse's relationship with relatives, and her attitudes towards
them. Relatives are often brought within the scope of the nurse's
communication tactics, as shown in the above example. A further
example demonstrates how nurses sometimes employ two sets of
tactics in one visit, one aimed at the patient, the other at the relative.

When a patient shows reluctance to accept more help, nurses
often use the tactic of making several brief references to such help
during the course of the visit, with the intention of letting the idea
take root. For example, in my study a senior nurse found one of her
female patients looking frail and ill one morning. The husband was
also ailing, and becoming less able to manage. The nurse promptly
offered a twice-weekly wash in addition to the injection, but the offer
was strongly declined and the matter was dropped. Five minutes
later the nurse mentioned it again in a slightly different way, with two
important underlying implications 'If at any stage you feel you
would like more help for a while, then don't hesitate to ask'. She was
implicitly allowing the patient to decide by suggesting that it was
her choice, and at the same time hinted it would be a temporary
arrangement.

When she was out of the patient's earshot the nurse spoke to the
husband, and mentioned the possibility of increasing the nursing
care. He wavered, and seemed uncertain, and nurse concluded very
firmly: 'From my experience it would be a very good idea'. By this,
she told me afterwards, she intended to put the onus on the husband
to persuade his wife to accept more help. Her tactics worked, and her
visits were increased at the wife's request.

Another nurse spoke of the importance of relationships with
relatives as a means for gathering extra information, or, simply 'the
other point of view'. Any situation in which one person is dependent,
and another is making considerable sacrifices to provide care and
attention is fraught with stress. Relatives may have problems in
judging how best to divide their time fairly between an elderly or ailing dependent, and their own family. District nurses gain a great deal
of experience and understanding of these sorts of problems and can
help relatives to resist excessively selfish demands.

Where there is continuing conflict between patients and relatives
the nurse's attitudes to the patient can be subtly affected, especially

where she is the guest in the relative's house rather than the patient's own home. She can afford to let the 'nurse' role be dominant and this might extend to denying the patient any opportunity to grumble or complain. At other times, however, nurses may act more as 'mediators' between the two sides, listening to points of view which might not be openly expressed, and then voicing them to the other party. In this way, the nurse can help understandings and reconciliations to take place within the households they are visiting.

Avoiding involvement

The nature of a district nurse's work means that she will inevitably come to know and understand some of her patients and their families quite intimately. She has to learn to discriminate between acceptable and unacceptable patient demands for her time and attention. In other words, she must know when to become involved in one problem and when to dismiss another. For example, I observed some nurses ignoring hints or clues from patients which indicated that the patients were seeking some kind of further help or attention. It is significant that this avoidance was confined to patients who were relatively independent, or had self-limiting problems. So when a nurse ignores a plea for attention, she may be quite consciously, and correctly, effecting a scale of priorities, since those patients who are highly dependent or very ill warrant the most attention. In order to allow sufficient time for this, nurses cannot afford to get waylaid, and the following example illustrates this.

> One of the nurses I was studying was pressed for time, and she was just concluding a relief visit to a female patient with a varicose ulcer. As she was putting on her coat the patient said she was very worried about the pain she was having, and her lack of improvement. The nurse dismissed this with: 'That's quite usual with ulcers'. She paused briefly, and abruptly said 'What a beautiful carpet you've got.' The patient was nonplussed. She made some comment about the carpet and then fell silent. The nurse said 'Well I must be going. Your own nurse will probably come next time'.

Outside the patient's house the nurse discussed her approach with me without any prompting. She said: 'I didn't want to get involved there. She had plenty of chance to complain while I was doing the dressing. It's amazing how so many of them try to delay you just as you're about to leave'. This nurse may have been right and she may have been wrong. Some patients are well known for their tendency to use these tactics, while others take time plucking up the courage to ask even one question. Until the nurse has known her patient long enough to judge the validity of pleas for help, it is obviously unwise for her to completely ignore any such clues or hints.

Coping with illness at home

Community nurses visit many different households during the course of their work, and in many of these, the nurse shares responsibility for the patient's care with spouses or other relatives. They manage the problems of caring for a sick or elderly person in a range of different ways, but I have found that nurses tend to categorise relatives as one or other of two possible stereotypes – they are either seen as 'copers' or 'non-copers'. The nurse's communication with families varies according to which of these two stereotyped categories she places the relatives in.

It is inevitable that people will have different methods of adapting to the same stress. In my study, a number of adaptations or 'coping mechanisms' were used by the relatives in response to the stress of caring for the sick at home. These were as follows:

they enlisted the support of other family members, so that work was shared;

they undertook the nursing but shared the problems with nurses and doctors in discussion; and

more rarely, they reduced the patient to a state of complete dependence, like a child.

All these 'coping mechanisms' were recognised and discussed by the nurses.

In what ways, then, did relatives fail to cope, and did these 'non-copers' fall into any specific group? All nurses described certain relatives as 'not coping' when there was evidence of patient neglect. It is perhaps significant that in the few cases where neglect was observed, all the patients involved had suffered a stroke. Some relatives cope with this inevitable trauma to the marital relationship by treating the sick spouse as a child. Others choose to turn away from the painful change that has been wrought in their lives, and consequently they neglect the patient.

It is worth considering why nurses describe 'neglect' as 'not coping'. This is an important issue because it shows how in-built attitudes and assumptions can prevent nurses from giving the most practical advice which could be given to families in difficulty. One starting point is the fact that almost everyone holds values about caring for the sick, and to most people it seems unnatural and inhuman to neglect a patient. 'Neglect' is not acceptable to most nurses, and strong professional and societal norms reinforce the desirability of 'good nursing care'. Since 'neglect' is rarely recognised as an adaptation process, it is tempting for the community nurse to stereotype such relatives as 'non-copers' and regard them as 'failures'. The nurses' actions in this situation are geared to reminding relatives of the role expected of them and to pointing out more appropriate methods of caring for the patient, rather than discussing fully the problems which the relatives themselves find most pressing. As has already been seen, attempts to point out and correct 'failings' may be greeted with hostility, but mostly the reaction is apathy. The following example demonstrates the latter reaction.

> One home where the wife was neglecting her husband was visited by a number of nurses, and many of them expressed their disapproval of this state of affairs. Their feelings were understandable since clean clothes were never put out, the house smelt of stale urine, and the husband always looked unkempt with trails of spilt food down his shirt-front. Most of the nurses' remarks to the wife referred explicitly or implicitly to her 'failings'. However, one day while the nurse was giving a bed bath and chatting to the patient, the observer overheard a conversation between the wife and a visitor just outside the bedroom door. The wife tearfully explained how the continual washing was 'getting her down', that meal times were a trial because his eating habits nauseated her, and his double incontinence disgusted her.

In the context of these remarks, 'failing' to put out clean linen was actually a means of coping with the excessive burden of washing, and it can be surmised that little or no supervision at meal times was this lady's method of coping with some of the unfortunate disabilities that follow a stroke. It appeared that the wife's 'neglect', and the consequent disapproval expressed by the nurse acted as a barrier to any fruitful discussion about how she could be helped to overcome her difficulties.

The fact that this barrier did exist was demonstrated when it was discovered that no one had suggested substitution of a feeding cup for an ordinary cup. This is not so much criticism of the nurses observed, as an illustration of the need for community nurses to be aware of the complexities and reasons for a phenomenon such as 'neglect'. If nurses were taught to regard an old lady's sad neglect of her husband as one among several alternative coping mechanisms that relatives can adopt, then their communication with both patient and relative might be much more effective.

Summary and conclusions

This chapter has taken an overall view of the whole process of communication between district nurses and patients who are being cared for in their own homes. There are two important lessons to be drawn. Firstly, the *role* which a nurse adopts when dealing with the patients and relatives she visits can considerably affect communication. It is important to recognise that nurses may not always choose this role, but that within each home they have to balance it carefully between 'guest' and 'nurse'. Awareness of the role the nurse is taking can bring new insights into the nurse/patient relationship in the community. In particular, it becomes possible to recognise the effect that adopting either the 'nurse' role or 'guest' role can have on the effectiveness of any given communication or longer term relationship with the patient.

Secondly, it is important to recognise the use of *tactics* – the skills and manoeuvrings that both nurses and patients use to get what they want, or to cope with situations involving illness and stress. Once again the aim of this chapter has been to enhance nurses' awareness and understanding of the existence of these tactics, especially in terms of the effect they can have on communication between themselves and their patients. No attempt has been made to suggest whether any particular roles or tactics are right or wrong. However, decisions must be taken about what kinds of communication tactics are called for by the needs and circumstances of individual patients cared for at home. One way of recognising these tactics is through careful analysis of nursing incidents such as those described in this chapter. This kind of systematic thought and analysis of particular incidents should be undertaken formally in training programmes, and informally by individual community nurses. In this way, one of our most important skills – that of communicating with patients – will cease to be ignored and regarded as entirely intuitive, and we can begin to develop it in order to achieve better patient care.

References

Altschul A. T. (1972) *Patient-Nurse Interaction.* University of Edinburgh Department of Nursing Studies, Monograph No. 3 Edinburgh: Churchill Livingstone

Hawthorn P. J. (1971) *The Nurse Working With the General Practitioner. An Evaluation of Research and a Review of the Literature.* DHSS London: HMSO

Johnson W. L. & Hardin C. A. (1962) *Content and Dynamics of Home Visits of Public Health Nurses.* American Nurses' Foundation

Korsch B. M. & Negrete V. F. (1972) Doctor-patient communication. *Scientific American,* August

Ley P. & Spelman M. S. (1967) *Communicating with the Patient.* London: Staples Press

McIntosh J. B. (1975) *An Observation and Time Study of the Work of Domiciliary Nurses.* Unpublished PhD thesis, University of Aberdeen

McIntosh J. B. (1979) The nurse-patient relationship. *Nursing Mirror,* **148** (4)

Chapter 8: Communicating with Cancer Patients

This chapter takes a social scientist's view of the complexities of communication in nursing. Therefore, in many respects the approach is similar to that of the previous chapter, although here the concern is with patients who have cancer. The particular anxieties generated by a diagnosis of cancer are described and analysed in relation to their effect upon the patients, their relatives and the nurses who care for them. The very widespread existence of these anxieties generates, in turn, a need for rapport, empathy and certain other specific communication skills on the part of nurses. However, society's attitude towards cancer brings special problems such as fear and repression which need to be recognised and understood before communication between nurses and patients can improve.

In this chapter, the author outlines and discusses the kinds of 'coping strategies' adopted by cancer patients in an attempt to come to terms with their illness, and some examples are given of patients who have adopted such coping strategies. In addition, the strategies which nurses use in their dealings with cancer patients are described, and the point is made that these often involve avoidance and uncertainty.

At some time or other, every nurse will care for patients with cancer, and the ideas expressed in this chapter should be relevant to a variety of different nursing situations. Many of these ideas are quite complicated and sophisticated, and readers should not expect this chapter to provide immediate solutions to all the problems in this difficult area of communication with patients.

Senga Bond completed her nurse training at the Western General Hospital, Edinburgh. She then worked there as a staff nurse in the radiotherapy unit before embarking upon academic studies at the University of Strathclyde which led to BA and Master's degrees in psychology. She was subsequently awarded a PhD at the University of Edinburgh. As well as pursuing her research on patients' adjustment to cancer, her current interests include research utilisation, and the management of pressure sores.

Chapter 8

Communicating with Cancer Patients

Senga Bond

Introduction

Patients with cancer pose special, different, and challenging problems when it comes to communication. This is because cancer is unique among illnesses in the kinds of deep rooted fears and anxieties it provokes. It is not just 'having cancer' that is stressful to the patient and his family but all that is associated with it, such as invalidism, pain, wasting, disfigurement, and death. Nurses, as human beings, are also affected by these feelings, and patients with cancer are to be found in almost every hospital ward. It is a disease which is also found amongst many of the patients attended by community nurses and there can be few students embarking on nursing training who do not very quickly encounter difficulties in communicating with cancer patients.

These connotations of cancer are not surprising, given society's attitude towards this disease, the hushed tones in which cancer is discussed and the greater emphasis generally given to death from cancer than to its cure. Although there have been dramatic improvements in treatment, in England nearly 120,000 people still die annually of cancer (DHSS 1978). Such bald mortality statistics reveal nothing of what it is like to have cancer in the family. District nurses reported the physical and mental suffering experienced by the majority of patients (Marie Curie Memorial Foundation 1952), and more recently Cartwright *et al* (1973) found that 87% of people dying with cancer at home reported pain, often of a distressing nature. Those who have cancer, as well as those who care for them, hold beliefs about the illness which are often determined by past experience as well as by what they have heard and read.

It is worth stating here that although 'cancer' is being treated as a single disease in this chapter, the term encompasses about 100 different illnesses each with varying prognoses and different

117

problems. For example, it has been shown that patients with breast cancer (Quint 1963; Maguire 1977) encounter unique problems which are quite different, for example, from those of patients with maxillo-facial cancer (Rosillo *et al.* 1973).

Writing about communication with cancer patients is described by Brewin (1977) as 'walking into a minefield of misunderstandings', and a great deal more of what has been written represents opinion rather than fact. This paucity of research is not surprising since the subject of cancer and its human response is as emotion-laden to investigators as it is to nurses, patients and their families. Quint (1963), for instance, found that nurse researchers studying the impact of mastectomy became so emotionally involved that they too needed help in dealing with their own feelings. If this is the case for research workers, it is even more true for patients who actually have cancer, and the nurses who care for them.

Coping strategies

In this chapter the task of communicating with patients suffering from cancer is discussed in terms of the 'coping strategies' which individuals use to come to terms with their illness. Weisman (1979) defines coping as 'what one does about a problem in order to bring about relief, reward, quiescence and equilibrium'. This definition illustrates three essential elements of coping. The first is the recognition of a problem from which relief is sought; the second is what the patient does (or does not) do about the problem, in other words, just how he copes, and the third aspect is an outcome, good, bad or indifferent, but offering no real guarantee about the long-term effectiveness of the coping strategy. Thus the concept of coping has important implications for cancer patients and the nurses who care for them, and is particularly relevant to the concept of communication.

Some writers have described how individual patients adjust to and cope with illness in different but quite consistent ways (Lipowski 1970). The manner of coping appears to depend upon a number of different factors. Hinton (1973), has suggested that some factors come from 'within the patient', and include personality, character, how they have coped with other stress in the past and their current feelings and beliefs about illness in general and cancer in particular.

Recognition of the patient's concerns and the extent to which strong and warm relationships exist between the patient and the people with whom he has contact also affect a patient's ability to cope. Social variables such as work and finance are also important. Interacting with all these are the disease factors themselves – diagnosis, site of malignancy, symptoms and prognosis – and with so many factors affecting the patient it is inevitable that coping will be unique to the individual.

Weisman (1976) has identified several different and enduring ways in which patients can cope. These he calls 'coping strategies', and while highly individualistic they do have certain common patterns.

The most common coping strategies are listed below:

. . . . the patient may:
1 Seek more information
2 Talk with others to relieve distress
3 Laugh it off
4 Not worry but try to forget
5 Put his mind on other things
6 Undertake some kind of positive constructive action based on his present understanding
7 Accept his position but rise above it and find something favourable
8 Show stoic acceptance of the inevitable
9 Do something, anything, however reckless or impractical
10 Do things which have worked for him in other situations
11 Reduce his own tension by drinking or taking drugs
12 Go away by himself
13 Blame someone or something for his condition
14 Seek direction and do what he is told
15 Blame himself and atone or sacrifice something

These strategies can change over time since coping is a dynamic process rather than an isolated activity (Lazarus 1966); so the strategies a patient uses may well develop and change over the course of his illness. However, it is also important to remember that patients do not leave all of their other concerns behind them when they develop cancer. They continue to have problems and concerns about, for example, a wayward son, a precarious job or a doubtful faith while they also are trying to face a diagnosis of cancer and its implications. It takes skill and time to accommodate such issues when assessing patients.

In order to learn how patients are coping with cancer we must learn more about their own concerns and worries. Some information can be obtained from observation and some from other people, but it is more effective to ask the patients themselves. There is often a reluctance amongst nurses really to encourage patients to voice their concerns but there is no other way of knowing what they might be. It is obviously difficult to prescribe a set of standard questions for cancer patients but the following kinds of queries* could be raised at most stages of a patient's illness:

1 What sorts of things are you worried about in, say, your life at home now that you know you are ill?
2 Have you got any ideas about how you might be able to cope with them?
3 How do you generally deal with big problems like these?
4 How does it usually work out?
5 Is there anyone you usually turn to when you need help like this?
6 What has happened in the past when you have asked for help like this?
7 Are there any particular problems which have tended to get you down in the past?

It is not feasible here to go into the detail of the actual words which can be used when asking patients about their concerns and worries. Further guidance is available elsewhere (Moos 1974) but even without an explicit set of ideas as to what should be asked, the list above can provide an opportunity for the patient to talk and let the nurse know his really pressing concerns. It is important to realise that patients' concerns can change quite quickly. How the patient views his plight can change even over a few days, and so continuity in assessment will assist in understanding and developing a helpful relationship with patients.

It is unusual for patients to rely on a *single* coping strategy. More commonly they intermingle, as illustrated by examples of patients I have known, and some of the coping strategies they employed. The

*This list is adapted from Weisman (1976)

patients I observed in a study carried out in a radiotherapy department (Bond 1978) demonstrated the use of several methods of coping, and examples of these are given below:

> One patient demonstrated strategies 1 and 2 (above). She was a very self-reliant spinster who had a carcinoma of the rectum. She had had a busy working life and gave up work to care for her father until he died. She had been treated surgically for haemorrhoids (whether or not this diagnosis was correct is uncertain) but further problems resulted in more surgery. She asked for her diagnosis and was told she had cancer. When her symptoms persisted she was referred for combined chemotherapy and radiotherapy. Her initial rationalisation that her symptoms were due to the aftermath of surgery had later given way to her understanding that the cancer was spreading. Now she wanted to know what her chances were and what the outcome of treatment would be. She asked the doctors and nurses, but it took great perseverance to obtain any answers. She also talked a lot with her fellow patients although she was not reassured by their responses any more than she was by those of the staff. She was helped by talking but also wanted frank information.

Another patient used strategy 7 (accepting but finding something favourable)

> This deeply religious 55-year-old woman was aware she had breast cancer. Her mother had died painfully of bowel cancer, after a short illness. The patient came to the hospital with severe pain due to metastic spread to one leg. Initially, she attempted to disassociate her leg pain from breast cancer although she was aware that spreading was a possibility. For a while she attributed it to a venous problem. But even if it had spread, she was content in having lived a good life. She was grateful that prompt attention to her breast lesion had 'given her a number of years' which was something denied to her mother. She did not yet want to die but she was not afraid of death, indeed her faith had been strengthened.

Determining the way a patient is coping demands accurate observation and effective listening on the part of the nurse, as well as the ability to interpret what is being said. Listening, therefore, has to be active rather than passive – in other words it should encourage further communication. Communication should be supportive, and if so, it will facilitate the patient's ability to cope. However, this does not always happen in practice. For example, the first patient above who asked for information and talked a lot was labelled by the nurses as 'Mrs Twenty Questions'. However, her persistence in asking questions was largely attributable to not getting any answers. The staff tended to avoid her physically as well as verbally. By telling the patient 'not to worry', they had not given her sufficient information to enable her to use her former tactics of independence, self-reliance and assertiveness. She could not establish a sound basis on which to make decisions and she could not tolerate the uncertainty. Her need to talk was expressed to other patients, and was exacerbated by the nurses avoiding her. Rather than enlisting the nurses' help she had managed to alienate them, and then later, her fellow patients. Nurses had interpreted her behaviour in terms of its nuisance value *for them* rather than its meaning for the patient. It is important therefore to try to understand what lies behind any patient's communication with staff and others.

This wider view of the meaning of communication is important in gaining an understanding of how any patient is coping. Some patients grumble, but in reality this may be an angry expression against the illness rather than against the staff. It is little wonder that a patient who is admitted for treatment for a carcinoma of the cervix, and who has a healthy bowel, resents having her bowel insulted to the extent that a colostomy is performed. People who value cleanliness and are fastidious are often disgusted by their own bodily products. They may then blame others for this predicament. Seen in this light, there is often a logic about complaints concerning food, sheets, service and so on. Such communication does create difficulties for nurses, but with understanding and suitable nursing interventions, patients can be helped to cope more effectively. Similarly, when a patient makes light of his illness, by joking and laughing, we should not assume that he underestimates its severity. This may be his way of coping with a harsh reality of which he is only too well aware. This joking approach (listed as strategy 3) may be easier for nurses to facilitate than some others, but the patient's needs must be taken seriously.

Hope and trust

Hope, uncertainty and denial are useful concepts in understanding how patients cope with cancer. Hope is rather intangible but

McIntosh (1977) identified how doctors and nurses interpreted their communication with cancer patients as aiming to sustain the patients' hope. Nurses also provided this explanation when I asked why they persistently avoided discussing the patients' illness and concerns. Nurses thought that to talk about the illness would be harmful to patients, encouraging depression and morbid attitudes and destroying hope. They feared precipitating what they regarded as harmful responses – weeping or other emotional outbursts, or even suicide. Crying patients were said to be upsetting to the nurses and the other patients, and destroyed the equilibrium of the ward.

However, hope appears to be a consistent and stable characteristic of patients with even serious illnesses. Stotland (1969) considers it to be a response which is learned through past behaviour, and reinforced by other people's support. Thus, as well as being dependent upon the patient's own resources, hope depends on the patient's social context and other supportive relationships.

Hope does not always rest in cure or even extended life. In my own research I found that patients engaged in limited goal-setting. They hoped that they would be able to manage at home; or walk without support; or that there was something more that could be done. Even when there was no hope of cure or recovery, patients are not necessarily pessimistic. They may hope that they will not have to suffer pain. In view of this it is not surprising that the absence of trust and hope often brings bitterness and despair. Enhancement of hope therefore demands an understanding of the basis of a particular patient's hope. Hope cannot be created by false reassurances, platitudes and deceptions about the future. Rather, these undermine trust and may undermine the quality of remaining life. A well-meant but false description of what is likely to help the patient can easily destroy trust and, with it, hope. To avoid this it is essential to give time to allow patients to express their concerns. Unfortunately, nurses are sometimes tempted to encourage optimism regardless of circumstances, and this can have dubious effects. One nurse said:

> 'It's only natural instinct to talk about the future and how things can only get better. I know Mr Graham isn't going to live but why depress him? If you talk about their holidays and the like, well, they feel they've got some future, something to live for. It's only natural instinct to think this way.'

This patient, however, knew his days were numbered and said to me

> 'Why do they try so hard to be cheerful? Would it not be better for us all if we dropped the pretence and somebody would show some interest in how I really feel.'

Hope is sustained by confidence and trust in others. This means that nurses should communicate with patients so that trust is engendered. If a nurse tells a patient 'not to worry' then this must be followed up by 'because – – –'. It also means providing answers which embody the truth without brutality. A combination of hope and trust is much more helpful to the patient who is trying to come to terms with the truth than is encouraging false optimism. Both doctors and nurses do at times rely on false optimism and this is associated with their feelings about the dangers of destroying hope and also with problems of uncertainty about the patient.

One ward sister in my study said:

> 'I find it difficult to communicate with them not knowing what they understand, what they've been told, what they want to know, what they would like to be told or what their relatives know and they want to happen.'

This tied in with nurses' stated fears of overstepping professional boundaries. Telling the patient his diagnosis was regarded in my study and in others (Quint 1963; McIntosh 1977) as the doctors' sole prerogative. This assertion, interestingly enough, was not upheld for non-malignant diseases (Bond 1978). Because nurses feared being asked for a diagnosis or prognosis, the range of other issues that nurses enquired about or in which they were otherwise involved became very limited. Most patients do not ask nurses for diagnostic information, but even if they did there is, in theory, little to prevent the nurse acting as a 'go-between' between patient and doctor. This would help the doctor to deal with the patient's need for information at any particular time.

Uncertainty

Patients with cancer must contend with uncertainties about their illness and future to a greater extent than in most other medical conditions, but it is important to realise that uncertainty is difficult to tolerate at any time. For cancer patients this is especially the case, yet nurses may feel that by maintaining a level of uncertainty, they are in effect keeping the options open and contributing to the patient's hopes about the future.

Information-seeking associated with uncertainty has been studied by McIntosh (1977) and also in my own research (Bond 1978). It was evident in these studies that finding out about the illness and the significance of symptoms or implications of treatment is not so much a matter of asking direct questions as gradually piecing together fragments and cues collected from observation of what was happening as well as what is said about the other patients and their tests or treatments. Of course, what is not said is often as significant as what is said (Weisman 1972; Renneker & Cutler 1952) and the expression and demeanour of staff provide cues to the alert patient.

Denial

Patients often attempt to put together a coherent picture of their present conditions and future prospects. This is sometimes achieved by selectively seeking and avoiding particular types of information, and then interpreting cues in the environment such as changes in treatment plans, readmission to hospital, or increased white blood cell monitoring.

Some patients want to establish the facts. Others seek and interpret information so that it nullifies any intolerable realities. Information is then reinterpreted in a way which is compatible with what the patient *can* accept. This process can take different forms one of which is called 'denial'.

We all engage in denial and it is not difficult to identify it among staff and patients. For example, the patient who rationalises – 'If there was anything wrong, the doctor would have told me. Now he hasn't, so I am just going along with the idea that everything is all right!'

Up to a point, it is relatively easy for nurses to encourage patients' denial and fortify it in the belief that it will maintain hope. The problem is that when denial becomes the usual method or strategy used by nurses it is *not only the illness which is denied but the patients too*. An extreme example may illustrate this.

> One middle-aged male patient with metastatic spread to his liver was scheduled one day to begin palliative treatment in an attempt to relieve

his symptoms. His condition had deteriorated rapidly over 24 hours, during which time his consultant who had planned the treatment had not seen him. He was close to death, and, because he was becoming restless and the nurses thought he would disturb the other young men in his room, he was transferred to a single room. The patient knew his death was near and asked that his wife be called. The nurse did this, but in the interim the porter arrived to take the patient for radiotherapy. The porter recognised that the patient was too ill to withstand all the movement involved but the nurse insisted that he was scheduled for treatment so he should have it. In consequence, the patient was taken down two floors to the treatment area where his consultant immediately recognised that he should not have been moved. He did not have treatment and died on arrival back at the ward without seeing his family.

On paper this affair sounds grotesque, but it exemplifies how the illness can become the primary consideration and the patient a very poor second.

In the above example, the patient had shown that he was aware of what was happening to him. Sometimes patients will use a combination of denial and awareness simultaneously. One female patient knew she had extensive metastatic breast cancer and yet she talked about beginning a new career as a writer. This would enable her to earn a living although she was physically weakened. In view of the equivocal information being given by nurses that she was 'responding well to treatment' that 'it takes time for improvements to show' the patient at this time opted for what *might be* rather than what *is*.

Patients can relate and respond differently to different people as Hinton (1973) pointed out. They may seek optimistic reassurance from one source while engaging in a more sombre exchange with another. This represents suppression rather than denial and can often be an attempt to protect a spouse, an elderly parent, or a child. It also often happens with staff. For example, I have observed a patient responding as if all was well with the nurses in the ward, giving no indications of her fears, yet seeking out the ward sister to confirm her suspicions that there was a metastatic spread through her lymphatic system. The ward sister acknowledged that the patient's interpretation was correct – she accepted the trust put in her, and she was secure enough to meet the patient's needs.

This suggests that it is important for staff to discuss the kinds of communication needed by different patients, in order to identify when they must establish different kinds of relationships. There are also implications for deciding when to assign particular nurses to work with particular patients in order to spend time with them and help them work through some of their problems.

The relationship between hope, uncertainty and denial

An understanding of the relationships between hope, uncertainty and denial are important in understanding nurse-patient communication in cancer nursing. Patients who exhibit high denial are often perceived as having fewer needs to know but they are *not* necessarily more hopeful. Silence and avoidance of the illness are *not* signs of acceptance any more than an open acknowledgement of cancer or a poor prognosis is a sign of potential suicide. Patients who are silent, who suppress their awareness or who cope through massive denial are usually regarded as uncomplaining and co-operative, freeing the nurse to care for others who are regarded as having greater needs. Unfortunately, because of the organisation of our health system, nurses in hospital who see patients for relatively short spells in the total course of their illness are encouraged to take only a short-term view. The longer perspective about denial as a method of adjustment to illness is that it can be unhelpful to patients. Cancer patients who use more positive strategies have been found to cope better (Weisman 1972). When there is both hope and trust there is strength enough to withstand the truth.

Some practical implications and applications

Throughout this chapter suggestions have been made about how nurses can communicate more meaningfully with cancer patients. Nonetheless, this cannot be a 'how to' chapter in the sense of offering universal advice to those who are nursing cancer patients. There are no easy solutions and no routines or set practices which can be slotted in. However, there are a number of suggestions which may increase nurses' effectiveness in their transactions with patients. Some of these apply to individual nurses, but there are also implications for the broader social system – the ward personnel and the school of nursing – in which nurses work. What the nurse learns in school will be of little help if she is not supported in practising it on the ward; and similarly, what the nurse learns of working with individual patients is unhelpful if she is not given the opportunity for any degree of continuity in working with the same patient.

Some suggestions for change have been outlined already but it is always useful to examine each individual situation and to identify which aspects may be ripe for modification, where weaknesses lie and where strength can be capitalised on.

Changes in nurse education   In my study I asked nurses about the kind of education they had received to enable them to communicate with patients. Some said they had received none, others referred to an introductory lecture or two in psychology. Some were surprised at the question, believing that there was no way in which communication could be taught – it depended on the individual patient and nurse. This suggests that attention is needed in teaching the difference between individualised care and interpreting an individual's needs so that appropriate care, derived from sound principles can be instituted. Principles of interviewing, assessment, interpretation, and of developing treatment plans can be applied to patients' psycho-social needs as well as to their physical needs. An introduction to communication skills, needed in order to assess and care for patients, can begin in basic education and be developed through post-basic courses. A useful exercise for tutors may be to examine the proportion of teaching time devoted to meeting the physical needs of cancer patients and that devoted to meeting psychological needs.

The importance of the ward sister cannot be overstated yet few have special training in communication with patients or practice in using the examples available in their wards to teach students. If the ward sister is insecure in her own communication skills, she will be unlikely to want to discuss these skills, or provide appropriate learning opportunities for students. Yet the ward sister who acts as a role model for future staff nurses must be a major source of informal learning in nursing communication.

My impression is that cancer nursing still ranks low in terms of how nurses generally regard the need for specialist preparation – the feeling is that anyone can do it because what is needed is primarily 'good basic care'. Nothing could be further from the truth, and the above statement depends on a very narrow definition of what 'good basic care' constitutes, relying predominantly on patients' rudimentary physical needs. If helping patients to deal with the despair of cancer is regarded as equally 'basic' in the patients' right to treatment, then the concept of cancer nursing becomes sophisticated and demands special training.

Change at ward or unit level In order that changes can occur, account must be taken of the social setting or 'milieu' of the ward. This milieu encompasses such factors as the relationships between nurses and doctors, between the nurses themselves, the organisation of ward work in respect of nurse-patient allocation; communication systems in respect of reporting and monitoring patient care and decision making. To assess these various factors in any situation where patients with cancer are being nursed, the following questions are worth considering:

1 Are policies clear with regard to what nurses should do if patients ask questions that the nurse feels incompetent, unwilling or unauthorised to answer?
2 Are formal or informal opportunities available for nurses who perceive particular communication problems with patients to enlist help? Are they used?
3 Is work arranged in such a way that if a patient-nurse relationship appears helpful, this can be fostered?
4 Are the mechanisms available for recording assessments of how a patient is coping and his point of vulnerability so that members of staff can keep up to date?
5 Do ward reports or team reports provide opportunities for nurses to share their assessments of patients and develop intervention plans?

Many of the above ideas require nurses to take increased responsibility for individual patients and their communication needs. However, the emotional demands which this will place upon nurses should not be underestimated, and it is important to ensure that any changes in nursing practice are accompanied by appropriate help and support for the nurses themselves.

Change for individuals If nurses are to develop effective communication expertise, whether in the context of coping with cancer or any other frame of reference, they will require certain knowledge, skills and attitudes. To obtain these requires a degree of motivation on the part of the nurse herself. It is essential to regard cancer nursing as more than just understanding the pathology and treatment, and being able to deal with the severe physical manifestations of the disease. It is more than just coping with a chronic disease; it is coping with the human consequences, misery and anxiety that cancer brings with it. Yet the human consequences are difficult for nurses to bear, and so personal resources and morale have to be developed and nurtured in those whose work entails extended periods with cancer patients. When all the nursing care seems to end in death, readmission for further treatment, disfigurement and misery it is not surprising that morale can be low at both an individual and group level. For this reason aspects of nursing which are morale-boosting – assisting patients to overcome problems, relieving some distress and recognising when good care has taken place need to be capitalised on, and success in assisting patients to cope more effectively should be included as an important learning experience. To do this, a technique known as process recording (Smith 1979) may be used to help nurses to develop awareness of their communication skills and deficits.

Summary and conclusions

This chapter has looked at the many different forms which communicating with cancer patients take. These result from the wide range of conditions and prognoses which come under the general heading 'cancer', as well as from the enormous range of strategies which patients evolve to cope with this disease.

One of the most widely encountered issues in patient communication involves the question: 'What should we tell cancer patients?' There is no simple answer to this problem for any member of the caring team, but clearer thought about each patient's capacity for hope; his tolerance of uncertainty; or his need for openness or denial should help in making individual decisions for individual patients. In order to reach this situation, in which balanced and informed decisions about nursing communication are arrived at for individual patients a great many changes are needed. These include changes at organisational, educational, and personal levels for nurses working with cancer patients.

Cancer care is amongst the most difficult and perplexing forms of nursing, since nurses have to face every day the progress of an apparently uncontrollable disease. In these circumstances it is easy to capitulate to the apparently insurmountable problems: to play it safe and not get involved, and to minimise the patient's needs. However, this chapter has tried to establish the fact that nurses involved with caring for cancer patients are far from helpless in the face of an advancing disease. Their contribution depends upon an appreciation of not only the physical problems, but also the social and psychological issues which are encountered by patients suffering from cancer. As a result, nurses should be able to develop ways of encouraging and maintaining the coping strategies which best suit individual patients. In the final analysis, many cancer patients need the nurse's ability for close and caring communication as much as any other aspect of her professional skill.

References

Bond S. (1978) *Processes of Communication about Cancer in a Radiotherapy Department.* Unpublished PhD thesis, University of Edinburgh

Brewin T. B. (1977) The cancer patient: communication and morale. *British Medical Journal,* **2,** 1623–1627

Cartwright A., Hockey L. & Anderson J. L. (1973) *Life Before Death.* London: Routledge & Kegan Paul

DHSS (1978) *On the State of the Public Health.* (Table L.6) London: HMSO

Hinton J. (1973) Bearing cancer. *British Journal of Medical Psychology,* **46,** 105–113

Lazarus R. (1966) *Psychological Stress and the Coping Process.* New York: McGraw-Hill

Lipowski Z. J. (1970) Physical illness, the individuals and the coping process. *Psychiatry in Medicine,* **1,** 91–102

McIntosh J. (1977) *Communication and Awareness in a Cancer Ward.* London: Croom Helm

Maguire G. (1977) The psychological and social sequels of mastectomy. In Howells J. G. (ed) *Modern Perspectives in the Psychiatric Aspects of Surgery.* Edinburgh: Churchill Livingstone, 330-421

Marie Curie Memorial Foundation/Queen's Institute of District Nursing (1952) *Report of a National Survey Concerning Patients with Cancer Nursed at Home.* London: Marie Curie Foundation

Moos R. (1974) Psychological techniques in the assessment of adaptive behaviour. In Coelho G., Hamburg D. & Adams J. *Coping and Adaptation.* New York: Basic Books, 334–399

Quint J. C. (1963) The impact of mastectomy. *American Journal of Nursing,* **63**(11), 88–92

Rossillo R. H., Welty M J. & Graham W. B. (1973) The patient with maxillofacial cancer –II– psychologic aspect. *Nursing Clinics of North America,* **8**, 153–158

Renneker R. & Cutler M. (1952) Psychological problems of adjustment to cancer of the breast. *Journal of the American Medical Association,* **148**, 833–838

Smith L. (1979) Communication skills. *Nursing Times,* **75**(22), 926–929

Stotland E. (1969) *The Psychology of Hope.* San Francisco: Jossey-Bass

Weisman A. D. (1972) *On Dying and Denying.* New York: Behavioural Publications

Weisman A. D. (1976) Coping behaviour and suicide in cancer. In Cullen J. W., Fox B. H. & Isom P. N. (eds) *Cancer, the Behavioural Dimensions.* New York: Raven Press, 331–341

Weisman A. D. (1979) *Coping with Cancer.* New York: McGraw-Hill

Weisman A. D. & Worden J. H. (1976) The existential plight of cancer: significance of the first 100 days. *International Journal of Psychiatry in Medicine,* **7**(1), 1–15

Chapter 9: Communicating with Dying Patients and Their Relatives

In the preceding chapter the special needs and anxieties of patients with cancer were examined in relation to their effect on communication between nurses and patients. However, while much of the anxiety felt by these patients may be related to their fear of possible death, for most of them, death remains a possibility rather than a certainty. In this the final contributed chapter of the book, we examine the problems that nurses can face when trying to communicate with patients for whom death has become an inevitability.

Care of the terminally ill is perhaps the most demanding of all areas of nursing. It can impose great emotional strain upon the nurses involved; and without experience, sensitivity and very specific skills it is difficult to communicate effectively with dying patients and their relatives. All these factors are recognised and discussed throughout this chapter, and the practical suggestions and hints given are based on the author's personal experience of nursing dying patients. Examples and anecdotes are also used to illustrate the various problems that nurses may encounter in communicating with the terminally ill and their relatives.

The author of this chapter, Maggie Hacking, trained at University College Hospital, London, where she subsequently worked as a staff nurse on a surgical ward and in the radiotherapy unit. She has since worked at St Christopher's Hospice, London, as a staff nurse, then as a Home Care Sister, and most recently with the bereavement visiting service.

Communicating with Dying Patients and Their Relatives

Maggie Hacking

Introduction

The vast improvements in medical knowledge which have taken place during the last fifty years have led to a society which tends to deny the existence of death and which does everything possible to disguise its reality. The emphasis of medical treatment and care is firmly directed towards prevention and cure, and death is no longer accepted as a normal part of family life as it was in previous generations. Indeed, it is often said that death has replaced sex as the taboo subject of our society. However, the care of the dying and bereaved is a field which in recent years has become a subject of real public and medical concern and, in consequence, the inadequate attention we give to the needs of the dying has been exposed.

Several researchers have investigated the stress and anxiety experienced by terminally ill patients and their relatives. Kubler-Ross (1973) has shown that such patients are often deeply afraid of loneliness and in consequence are in particular need of communication and support from those who are caring for them. She also describes the stages through which such patients appear to progress and suggests that if the process is anticipated by nurses and doctors appropriate advice and support can then be given. Saunders (1976) and Raven (1975) have also studied the problems faced by dying patients and they emphasise the need for sensitive and effective communication. In addition, Parkes (1972) has shown that bereaved relatives are in need of information and support for some time before and after death takes place. Avoidance of open communication can lead to dying patients being cared for in a deceptive and confusing atmosphere – what Glaser and Strauss (1965) term a state of 'closed awareness'. The findings from more recent research (McIntosh 1977; Bond 1978) suggest that doctors and nurses do use a variety of strategies to avoid communicating with terminally ill patients. Lack of communication can also result in patients receiving inadequate pain relief and attention to basic physical needs. Cartwright *et al.* (1973) demonstrated that advice, explanation and reassurance from doctors and nurses were absent in a large proportion of the cases they surveyed where death had occurred at home. The topic of communication is therefore vitally important when considering the nursing care of those who are terminally ill. It is however, a complex area and much affected by practical factors, the attitudes of patients and nurses and the atmosphere or philosophy of the environment in which the patient is being cared for.

Hospice, hospital or home?

Although many people express a preference for dying at home, the fact remains that the majority die in hospital or a hospice. The figures up to 1974 show that less than one-third of all patients dying from cancer, actually died at home (Table 9.1).

Table 9.1   Total deaths and percentage of deaths occurring in non-psychiatric hospitals (NHS and other) and at home – England and Wales, 1970–74 (Cancer deaths only)

	Total (1,000's)	*Non-Psych. Hosps.*	*Home*
1970	117	61·5%	33%
1971	118	63%	32%
1972	120	63%	31%
1973	121	63%	31%
1974	123	64%	31%

(from 'The Management of Terminal Disease'. Ed. Saunders (1978)

As can be seen from this table, most cancer deaths occurred in hospital and more recent statistics suggest that the proportion of patients actually dying at home continues to become even smaller. In 1977, of 126,000 cancer deaths, 68% occurred in non-psychiatric hospitals and institutions and 29·9% occurred in the patient's own home (OPCS 1979).

A recent trend has been the establishment of increasing numbers of homes or hospices specifically concerned with the care of the dying. Although a few of these have been in existence for many years, work in the field of terminal malignant disease, such as that pioneered by Cicely Saunders, has led to the setting up of many new terminal care units for such patients on a world-wide basis. The term 'hospice' has come to symbolise this new growth of terminal care (dictionary definition: 'travellers' house of rest'), although titles of units vary, and include, for example, Continuing Care Units, Palliative Care Units and Nursing Homes.

The philosophy behind the expansion of hospice care is the recognition of the need to provide facilities for the dying patient and his family, so that a caring and skilled team can share the management of the total care – dealing with the physical, mental, spiritual and social problems as they arise and change. Hospices have developed as separate institutions because it has been, and still is, difficult to integrate the slower pace of care and increased individual attention needed by the dying into busy general hospitals. As well as in-patient care, many of these units have a home-care programme working in conjunction with the local community services, enabling patients and families to be supported in their homes and to die at home if appropriate.

Such specialised units are making an undoubted contribution to our knowledge and understanding of the care of the dying, but the fact remains that at present the majority of patients do not die in hospices – they die either at home, in general hospitals, specialist cancer units or in geriatric wards. In consequence, most nurses are required to care for and communicate with dying patients and their relatives in circumstances which are often far from ideal.

Patients and relatives are often reluctant to reveal their distress to medical staff and this can leave the nurse with an additional responsibility to observe their needs. However, nurses are often constrained by a busy ward routine or an overloaded working day in the community and these constraints make it difficult to find time for communication with dying patients and their relatives. But the need for communication cannot be overemphasised and terminal care, therefore, presents a challenge to every nurse caring for dying patients whether in the home, or hospital or hospice.

The relationship of communication to physical care

Perhaps more than any other group of patients, the dying and their relatives are in need of skilled communication on an emotional, social and spiritual level. At the same time they often require extensive physical care and it is clearly not possible to communicate effectively unless these physical needs are met. Physical and mental pain are very closely linked and in practice it may be impossible to separate them because communication with the patient cannot easily develop while he is in physical distress. Adequate control of distressing symptoms can and must be achieved, but with this must come expert and sensitive nursing care, combined with careful observation so that any new symptom or change in condition can be treated. It is this attention to the smaller details which improves the quality of life for the dying person, for example, allowing him to retain as much independence as possible by placing things within his reach if he is very weak.

Anticipating needs is one way of ensuring that the patient will not have to call the nurse too frequently – a circumstance which can be demoralising. A welcoming atmosphere on admission also helps to set the tone for future relationships; a warmed bed, a friendly reception and time and attention for relatives all give the patient a sense of his own worth. The basis for all communication must be good physical care, and in carrying out this care the nurse is in a unique position to relate to the patient and thereby tend to his emotional needs.

The gradual development of a new philosophy of terminal care is bringing with it a change in attitudes and expectations. Death and bereavement are gradually becoming more openly discussed both in public and amongst individuals. Where this has happened, patients and families increasingly want changes to take place in the decisions made about treatment and care.

In order to become involved in such decisions, patients and relatives require adequate and appropriate information and a great deal of emotional support. These requirements mean that demands will be made upon the communication skills of nurses and doctors. Even more than that, nurses and doctors are in a position to change attitudes towards death and increase knowledge and understanding by reducing anxiety and fear. In consequence, great demands will inevitably be made on nurses – demands which are both practical and emotional. To communicate effectively and compassionately with the dying and the bereaved requires skill, patience and experience, and this chapter attempts to tackle just this situation. Parkes (1976) describes the problem as follows:

'Terminal care is a matter of human relationships. There are skills to be learned and insights which can be gained from reading books, but the challenge and the reward of terminal care arises from the fact that it demands that we use the whole of ourselves to relate to our fellow human beings who are in trouble. This can only be learned by experience in a community in which relationships are valued and fostered.'

Gaining confidence in communicating with dying patients and their relatives

The first step in communication requires the nurse to gain confidence in being with those who are undergoing the stress of facing terminal illness. It is a natural feeling to want to avoid such patients and their relatives – especially when there are others requiring attention who are easier to be with, and who do not ask awkward questions about their illness. To overcome this barrier it is necessary to learn to relate to such patients as individuals, remembering that the fact that they are dying does not deprive them of personalities, feelings or responses to life.

'Communication' by definition means an exchange between people, and for this to be effective a relationship must be established. As nurses I believe we are trained not to become 'involved' with our patients, but when working with those who are dying, a vital component of care is that those cared for should feel that they matter as people. It is worth considering how a nurse can be committed to her patients as individuals yet still find it possible to give 'professional' help. Firstly, it is necessary for us all to consider ourselves and where we stand as 'care givers'. In this connection, it is especially important to think about death, and what it means in personal terms.

Is the thought of death so devastating that when we meet it in others we are overwhelmed; or is it so distressing that we deny our feelings about it completely? It is easier to be with dying people if the inevitability of one's own death can be accepted, albeit in the strong hope that one can at present look forward to a full and useful life. In other words, a balanced outlook in the face of the distress of others will enable nurses to help patients make decisions and to be involved in their care in a rational, and therefore effective, way. Of course, this attitude cannot be perfectly maintained – everyone is bound to be more affected by certain patients, such as someone of a similar age and interests to themselves. The support of team colleagues is therefore essential if the care of such patients is to be shared.

Another reason why nurses may feel ill at ease with patients who are dying may result from a lack of opportunity to understand the needs and feelings which patients and relatives experience during the days or weeks of a terminal illness. Nurses can learn a lot from one particular group of patients – those who are diagnosed as having malignant disease – since there is usually a time or stage which can be recognised as terminal. This 'early warning' of impending death can give nurses time to learn how to recognise the communication needs of such patients and their families. When nurses have gained confidence in this area they will be able to help the patient and his family use their time constructively rather than just 'waiting to die'.

The communication needs of the dying patient and his family

The need for an appropriate environment An appropriate atmosphere is essential if any attempt to communicate with and support the patient and his family is to be successful. People cannot begin to express their feelings or explore their fears unless *they* feel that the time and the place is right. This means that dying patients must be given the time of others in order that confidence and security may grow. In theory, the patient's own home is likely to provide the most appropriate environment – assuming that necessary physical and medical care can be achieved. However, while there are many patients who do wish to remain in their own home, others feel safer in hospital. This is especially common when symptoms prove difficult to control or the illness causes family tensions to grow. When patients are dying in hospital, the onus is upon the nurses to work towards providing an appropriate environment. This means helping patients and relatives to feel in tune with their unfamiliar surroundings, and it is specially important for the nurse to reassure them that they are not a hindrance or a nuisance to the ward routine.

However, it is often simply impossible to maintain an overall peaceful atmosphere on a busy general ward. Therefore it may be more practical to consider ways in which individual dying patients can be helped to feel calm or at ease by the nurses' attitudes and behaviour. In this context, the importance of a personal and warm welcome for patients and relatives on admission cannot be over-emphasised. These first impressions set the tone for all future interactions between the nurses and the patient. Relatives must be made to feel welcome; comfortable facilities and as much privacy as possible should be provided, and they should also be assured that they can visit whenever they wish. The maintenance of privacy is an important factor because dying patients often feel that they have lost their dignity due to changed appearance or complete weakness.

Although it is obviously easier to adapt the ward routine to an individual patient's need in a specialised unit, the terminally ill *can* be successfully and sensitively nursed in diverse situations. It is important to remember that the dying patient needs to be helped to *live* as he wishes. This may mean taking part in the normal ward activities such as eating at table, or going to occupational therapy. The whole ward team has to work together to provide the right balance of care for each individual patient.

The need to talk   There can be no firm rules about how you can recognise when a patient or relative needs to talk. It is not possible to goad people into talking because someone else thinks it is the right thing for them to do – you can only try to learn to take the lead from them. In fact for nurses, 'listening' is often a more appropriate concept than 'talking', but it is a discipline which can be hard to learn and difficult to achieve. Most of us are prone to filling a silence with our own words rather than waiting for the patient to continue.

Patients know which nurses they feel they can talk to most easily, and which ones have the time and inclination to listen. It is important not to overlook facial expressions or a seemingly innocent comment which may be the introduction to a deeper conversation. For example: a patient being washed, might say, jokingly 'Not much good, am I today nurse? – I could do this for myself last week'. At this point the nurse has a choice about how to respond. She could simply give light-hearted but false reassurance or she could give the patient an opportunity to develop the conversation by replying for example, in the following way – 'Well, you know we can always help you, but it is a worry isn't it, when you feel weaker? Do you worry a lot?' If the patient wants to talk further then the nurse should feel free to sit quietly and listen.

Although it is important to feel that nurses have a responsibility to enable the patient to talk if he wants to, it is necessary to recognise that each person has a different way of expressing himself. Some may talk quite frankly to a member of staff that they trust, whereas others may only want to touch the subject lightly or obliquely. It is necessary therefore to resist any temptation to 'force' a patient to open up a conversation. Even those who talk frankly on one occasion may need to be denying a few days later, and relatives, as well as staff, need to understand this.

The sort of topics that patients and their relatives often want to discuss vary greatly and can range from the practical details of care to the sort of deep fears described later in this chapter. It is vital, therefore, to find out exactly what the problem or worry is. It may be something which seems very minor, but nevertheless is causing great anxiety – in this case reassurance may be easier than expected. On the other hand, they may need expert advice with regard to social or family problems, or with making a will, or they may have spiritual needs which require discussion with a priest. The nurse's ability to sense any need and to give initial help is crucial to good care and can facilitate some resolution of problems where time is short.

The need to be told the truth   We are all familiar with the loaded question 'Should the patient be told the truth?' Of course, there can be no hard and fast answers to this question; in fact, the question itself is deceptive and grossly oversimplified. We cannot ever assume that a patient does not 'know' and this is even true of dying children (Bluebond-Langner 1978). If the patient's condition is obviously deteriorating he will be aware that things are not as they should be in spite of treatment. At this stage a decision to tell *him* nothing but to inform his relatives fully only serves to isolate him from those nearest to him and from those who are caring for him. This, unfortunately is still common practice, and results in a 'conspiracy of denial' from the beginning which nearly always leads to further complications and deceptions. However, there are many changes taking place in the way in which we deal with the problems of 'telling the patients the truth'. These changes are occurring in response to the change in social attitudes to death discussed earlier in the chapter and in response to a growing awareness amongst doctors and nurses of the need to acquire skills and experience in 'telling'.

Who should tell?   It should be made clear that in this instance we are talking about the discussion with the patient of the prognosis, rather than the initial diagnosis, although there are times when the two are synonymous. Perhaps 'tell' is the wrong word, because it is not an isolated happening where the patient is told everything. Rather it should be a careful imparting of truthful information as the illness progresses and the situation changes. Naturally it is the doctor's duty to take a leading part in the giving of this information, having first consulted the relatives as to whether they too want to take some part in it. However, relatives are sometimes determined that the patient should not be told of a poor prognosis. It is then the task of the ward staff to try to show that the patient is more likely to be helped by honesty rather than by a conspiracy of silence. Once again it is the nurse who finds herself spending most time with the patient, and playing an important part in this process.

After the patient has had the chance to think over information from the doctor, the nurse may well be the one who has to deal with remaining doubts and questions. So, as well as being aware of what the patient has already been told, she needs the freedom to be able to enlarge upon information given, and if possible, to deal with any new questions which may arise. The doctor in charge, hopefully, will be prepared to give her this freedom, knowing that she will report back to him and refer to him any question that she feels unable to cope with.

When to tell?   The responsibility for deciding when 'to tell' most commonly falls to the doctor although he may ask the nurses' advice on the matter. There is of course no firm answer to this question. There may be times when a patient has to be told that he has not long to live, because he has responsibilities which have to be dealt with, such as arrangements for the care of young children or elderly dependents. Generally, though, a good rule is to wait for the patient to ask – or tell you. Questions usually come up as problems arising out of the illness, for example, when a new symptom leads to further treatment, or increasing weakness. Again, the nature of the questions or comments vary with the personality of each patient, but there is no doubt that if patients really want their questions answered, they will choose a time when they and the nurse are alone and can have a conversation in privacy. The importance of not appearing to be in a hurry must be stressed and if, in a busy ward, there is an urgent call which cannot be ignored, it should be possible to find time to return to the patient later to try to pick up the conversation. The nurse's attitude should help the patient to share his anxieties, and if she can sit and relax with him and concentrate on him alone, then his confidence will grow.

All patients have the right to know what is happening to their bodies and what help is available, and nurses have to be sensitive as to how they want to use this right – if at all. The timing will depend upon the circumstances of their illness since sometimes if people are given too much information too soon, their hope can be destroyed to the extent that a long illness becomes very hard to bear. This can happen especially with those who are able to speak of their illness and death very openly from the beginning. On the other hand, it is essential that an atmosphere prevails where questions can be asked before the patient is so debilitated that he lacks the will to engage in such conversations.

When a patient has been told that he has a terminal illness When the time comes to talk to a patient of his impending death, it is important that the person doing so has already established a relationship with the patient. This will mean that the patient can enter into a dialogue with the doctor or nurse who should try to understand his particular needs, and assess how much he is ready to know. In most cases this information should be given gradually. No human being can be expected to come to terms with the full knowledge of his own death in one interview. Once the patient begins to realise the gravity of the situation he needs reassurance and hope that help can be given at all steps of his illness. Patients and relatives often say how difficult they have found the actual process of being given the painful information. To be told the truth bluntly in a busy out-patients department or ward can lead to unnecessary devastation and despair. Time must be allowed for the patient to talk about his fears and for the staff to reassure the patient about the continuing care he will receive.

Patients who are dying often feel that they are being written off and are no longer an interesting case. Some patients even feel they have to try and protect the doctor by showing courage rather than asking difficult questions and voicing their fears. Because the words we use to tell a patient about his poor prognosis are both difficult to comprehend and to accept it is better to proceed slowly, and even somewhat ambiguously if unsure, allowing the conversation to develop so as to respond to the patient's reactions. It is as well to remember that unwelcome news can so easily be misinterpreted, and many patients deny what they have heard. For this reason it is always worth retracing conversations to clarify points that may have been unclear or misconstrued.

The nurse's role as a communicator

As a general rule a nurse will not often be called upon to *inform* a patient or relative about the terminal nature of an illness in the first instance. Her role will most frequently be to repeat or reinforce any information given by the doctor, to give a careful explanation where the patient is unsure or confused, and to allow and encourage the patient and relatives to explore their problems, ask questions and so on. For this reason it is important that every nurse knows as much as possible about what her patient has already been told and how the patient was informed.

From this point on it is a nursing responsibility to assess how the patient and relatives have reacted to the information, and to assess their understanding of the situation and their need for further information, support, or time to talk. In my experience only a few patients will ask outright 'Is it cancer?' or 'Am I dying?'. In this situation I myself have not felt that it is right to answer directly with a 'yes'. It is usually best to respond to this question with another question to find out more of what the patient really wants to know, for example, 'What has the doctor told you about your illness?' or 'What makes you think that?'. This encourages a dialogue which can then make it possible to impart information in an acceptable way. The example might continue: 'The treatment was not as successful as the doctor hoped as no doubt you can tell from the way you feel – there is still some growth there which is causing you this pain. We cannot cure the illness, but there is a lot we can do to help the pain and help you to have a better quality of life'. It is also common, though, for the patient to tell *us* the situation if he is allowed to. For example, 'The doctor says it wasn't cancer, but I reckon he was wrong'. This statement perhaps asks for silent affirmation rather than a direct answer. It may be right to go on to say something like 'Well, there are lots of different types of cancer and they all behave differently. The drugs we use today can help people live with it, you know.' It is is difficult to be specific about this sort of answer, but perhaps the above examples give some indication as to how words can be used to the best advantage while adhering to the principle of honesty.

Nurses will often be asked *practical* questions about death and dying – questions which patients and relatives are loath to bother doctors with, but ones which in fact often relate to their deepest anxieties. It is essential therefore that every nurse should be prepared to try to talk about death and dying rather than evade the questions or avoid the issue. While one only learns to talk about such subjects by experience, the following points are worth remembering as they can be used in many situations. The patients and relatives are encouraged to communicate if they can be made to feel that they have the nurse's total attention and interest, and as much of her time as they need (although it may not feel like this to the nurse herself!) A quiet setting helps, if it can be arranged, where interruptions are minimised, and nurses should be allowed to sit on the patient's bed if this is the easiest way to talk to him. The nurse's posture and facial expression indicate a great deal to the patient about her reaction to what is being said. Embarrassment, for example, is easy for the patient to detect. A relaxed attitude showing acceptance and lack of embarrassment about a difficult subject should be worked at. Even an obvious thing such as direct eye contact can sometimes take an effort to achieve. Physical contact with the person who is supporting them can also be very comforting to the patient or relative, and may give them the courage to express painful feelings. Just a touch on the arm or hand may be enough. Sometimes when words are superfluous, it is easier to share fears by placing a comforting arm round the patient or relative's shoulder. People often need time to express what they want to say, and one of the hardest lessons to learn is to remain silent when patients hesitate or search for words. Silence makes most people feel uncomfortable and there is a tendency to fill silences with irrelevant words, which in fact only serves to inhibit the speaker. When giving information or advice, it is important to sound confident and if in any doubt about a particular problem it is better to say honestly that you need to discuss this with sister or doctor (or any other appropriate team member) first, rather than give an unsure, vacillating answer which will undermine the patient's confidence.

Questioning and reflecting   Although listening and 'being still' with the patient is essential, there are other skills which can be employed to help patients express the difficult things they may be trying to say. Just adding the right word, phrase or question to the conversation at the right time can make all the difference to the course it takes.

One of the most effective ways to promote such a conversation is to help the patient to reflect on what has been happening to him. Most people respond to this very readily and are obviously helped by talking back over their illness, or even about how they felt yesterday. For example, a patient may say 'I was all right after the operation, and I went back to work; then this pain came in my leg, but the treatment they gave me hasn't helped much – I suppose it will come right in the end'. At this point he seems to be asking a question which could be explored further, although it will soon be obvious if he does not want to do so. A possible interjection could be: 'You sound a bit doubtful, I expect this continuing pain is worrying you'. According to the reply, it may be possible, for example, to explain simply how the pain is being caused (eg. softening of the bone causing pressure on the nerve) and how it can be helped, as well as mentioning the fact that it is a condition that will need long-term care.

In other circumstances, a question asking the patient to develop what he has said may lead to him understanding or accepting his own situation a little better. A patient might say 'This illness has gone on so long, nurse – I can't see myself getting better now; I can't bear to think of the future'. By asking him what he fears especially about the future, it may become apparent that he is fearful of physical suffering, or being left alone, or even further treatment, rather than death itself. So it may then be possible to allay some of his specific fears, while still enabling him to begin to accept that he is dying.

Dealing with patients' and relatives' fears: the importance of listening and answering questions Patients of all kinds fear the unknown, and they fear that they may not be able to bear the physical and mental distress which may result from their illness. As nurses we should listen to them and find out exactly what they do fear, for we can usually give some assurance of help, and can tell the patient certain fears may be unfounded. A person who is showing anxiety may be difficult to communicate with, and it may be necessary to take the initiative and open up the conversation. There are techniques which nurses can use to help patients explore their problems and fears, and one method of doing this is shown in the following illustration.

Mrs A was being visited at home by a nurse from the home care team. She was withdrawn and abrupt in her greeting. She said that she had attended her treating hospital the previous day expecting further treatment for her deterioration, and none was forthcoming. The interview was brief:

Mrs A, angrily: 'After yesterday, I'm beginning to wonder where all this is going to end. Last time I had this pain, they cured it with treatment, and now they have given me these pills and they're no good at all.'

Nurse: 'It seems that you had a bad day yesterday Mrs A, what exactly happened at the hospital?'

Mrs A, near to tears: 'Well to be honest, nurse, it started off wrong. I met a lady I often see there and this time she really seemed very ill.'

Nurse: 'That must have been frightening.'

Mrs A 'Yes, she was in such pain and was so weak – I suppose that could happen to me.' Short silence, during which time nurse tried to show by her expression that she recognised what it was that Mrs A was trying to express, in other words that she was facing up to her own deterioration and death. The nurse then went on to give advice on how the new pills were to be taken and to assure the patient that pain can be controlled throughout an illness, and that care and support are available to people as weak as her friend.

This example demonstrates a number of points about communication. Firstly, the nurse could easily have responded to the initial anger by taking the first statement at face value; sympathising and going straight on to try to help the physical pain. However, she sensed that there was hidden fear and asked a question to find out more. In doing so, the nurse's attitude gave the patient confidence to express her fears. The patient knew that the nurse was trying to understand and was not frightened by what she was saying.

In the above example, the nurse felt that the patient was not ready to have her worst fears explicitly confirmed ('I suppose that could happen to me'), but her implicit confirmation helped Mrs A to face up to the situation and begin to accept it. To have denied the fears would have isolated the patient since the patient herself clearly knew what the situation was. Hope was maintained for Mrs A with the reassurance of pain control, and she was assured obliquely and by implication that she would be given full care to the end. During the course of her illness, Mrs A was able gradually to cope with more of the truth and, towards the end of her life, became able to talk openly about dying.

Fear is not something which shows itself constantly, but can take various forms, including denial, anger, depression and despair. Denial occurs even when the patient has been clearly told of his situation. Sometimes a patient will fluctuate between talking about his coming death, and about, say, next year's holiday. It is important to accept that this can happen and relatives must also have it explained to them. Even when a patient has not been told that he is dying, he should be given opportunities to talk generally about his condition. However, it is important to remember that there are some individuals who never want to talk or ask questions, or who never accept what they have been told even though most suspect the truth deep down. We must respect the fact that this is *their* way of coping.

Fear of death may also be expressed in anger by both patients and their families, and this often directed towards doctors and nurses. It is important to try to recognise the cause of this anger, allowing the person to work through it by expressing it and talking about what they feel. Many patients express their fear through depression and despair.

When the patient feels that all hope has disappeared he may ask 'What is there left to live for?' or 'Why don't you let me die now?'. These can be very difficult and threatening questions to answer and there is little value in trying to answer these questions logically, however sensible the answers may sound to us. The most helpful nursing tactic is perhaps to show the patient that we accept these awful feelings, and not try to counteract them with the reasoning of a healthy person. It may be right to say something like: 'Yes, I know that life seems purposeless for you now – pain and illness do make people feel like that, and it's almost impossible to fight against them alone'. However, if we can let patients know that they still matter as a whole person despite their sickness, some of their lost self-esteem may return.

If, as nurses we are aware of some of the specific fears and anxieties that patients and relatives may have, we will be much better equipped to help them talk about these fears.

Some of the fears patients most commonly express include:

1 the fears of physical distress and loss of independence and control already mentioned;
2 the fear of separation from familiar people and things:
3 the fear of not being able to achieve some life-long goal, such as a planned retirement or trip; and
4 the fear that death is some form of 'punishment'.

An illness like cancer, and death itself, can be seen by some patients as punishment for the way they have lived their life. It is surprising how many people say 'What can I have done to deserve this?'. Of course, if they feel they have failed in life this guilt is increased. It is important not to reject this out of hand since the guilt is very real for the patient. The presence of guilt may indicate a spiritual need and patients may benefit by seeing the hospital chaplain or their own priest if they express a wish to do so.

I have sometimes been asked 'Do you believe there is anything afterwards nurse?'. I am able to answer in the affirmative, but for a nurse who cannot, a possible answer could be 'I know that many people do but I must admit that I have difficulty with that idea – what do you feel?'.

Sometimes patients are fearful about the actual process of dying, and relatives especially will quite often ask directly 'What will the dying be like?' and 'what should I expect?'. They are also helped by knowing that the same nurses who cared for the patients will attend to his body after death. It is helpful to explain that most people slip into a deep sleep at the end, and that death itself is usually a very quiet event.

A real example may illustrate the point:

> The patient, aged 41 years, had been depressed, anxious and full of fear for her husband and 12-year-old daughter. She expressed a wish

to attend chapel services though she had not been a churchgoer, the spiritual comfort she desired obviously eased her anxiety. She asked a nurse 'What will happen at the end?'.

Answer from nurse 'Do you mean how will you feel?'.

'Yes.'

She was told that she would gradually get weaker and at the end would probably sleep most of the time, that she would not be left alone at the end and that any difficult symptoms could be controlled. She seemed reassured: later she said 'I am grateful to know how things are. It is much better than being patted on the head like a child'.

It is also worth mentioning to relatives that pain-relieving drugs often need to be given by injection rather than orally when the patient is near death. To relatives sitting by the bedside this procedure can easily be misinterpreted if not properly explained, and they may fear that their relative is being 'killed'.

One of the things that often causes both patients and relatives most fear and anxiety is what happens at the actual moment of death. This is especially true when patients are being cared for by relatives at home. There are several ways in which nurses in hospital can help to allay these anxieties. Even though a dying patient appears to be unconscious, sitting with him and maybe holding his hand demonstrates continuing support, and can also reassure other patients that they too will not be left alone. Although they may want to do so, families can find sitting with a very ill relative very difficult. Families often need encouragement and the nurses' reassurance that it is all right to read or chat quietly to each other, and they do need to know that conversation need not be necessary. For many relatives this may be their first experience of death or dying and the presence of a nurse sitting with them for a short time can help. Relatives may also need permission to leave the patient and attend to their own needs for a while, knowing that the nursing staff will call them if there is further deterioration. When the patient is being cared for at home, the nurse can help the family by giving them an explanation of what to expect over the coming days or weeks, and by providing a telephone number at which they can reach a nurse at any time.

Communicating with relatives The relatives and friends of a patient who is dying can be under immense strain. This strain is borne both of the distress and despair they feel about losing a loved one, and of their responsibilities for making decisions, and behaving in an appropriate fashion. Relatives are often told the bad news first and are asked there and then to advise the doctor whether the patient should be told. Of course, their initial reaction is often to protect their loved one and themselves from the pain involved in sharing the facts. If, as a family, they can be supported more by those caring for them, they can be helped to share the problems of terminal illness right from the start. Many families benefit from this approach, but we must respect those families for whom this sharing of knowledge and pain does not fit in with their usual way of coping with life.

Nurses are often involved in the conflict that relatives suffer because of differences in the knowledge of the current situation possessed by the patient and the relatives. Even if the patient knows the diagnosis and prognosis, it is likely that the relatives are able to be more realistic, as they can view the situation from the outside whilst being informed by the staff as the patient's condition changes. This inevitably means that there will be tensions within the family as relatives strive to contain their extra knowledge when they are with the patient. A nurse in close touch with the family can listen both to the relatives and the patient, in order to help each towards an understanding of the other's feelings and the state of their present knowledge. This may be done separately if, for example, the patient has indicated to the nurse that he realises he won't get better, then she is in a position to say to the relatives something like 'I think he is trying to make it easier for you, but he does seem aware of what is happening and was able to tell me so', thus reassuring them that if they are put in a position of having to show their feelings or talk about illness, the patient will probably be able to cope with it.

It may also be possible to bring a family closer together by sitting with the patient and his relatives, encouraging discussion about their mutual problems. For example, as an outpatient nurse, I visited a couple for the first time. The wife had met me at the door looking anxious and in a whisper urged me 'You won't tell him what he has got will you? He doesn't know how ill he is'. I assured her that I had come to help with symptoms and his care and not to tell him anything that he was not ready to know, although I would try to answer his questions honestly. The wife herself had diabetes which was poorly controlled and it seemed that her husband's care was proving too much for her: he seemed very weak and lay in a withdrawn or sleepy state most of the time. Throughout the interview the husband hardly responded to my presence although I tried to include him in the conversation. Eventually his wife and I were discussing the possibility of early admission as she felt she could cope no longer, when the patient sat up with difficulty and said bluntly 'You two may think you know everything, but I asked the doctor and was told I was dying nine weeks ago.' At this, the wife's emotions came to the surface with tears and they began to comfort each other. I felt very superfluous and decided to go, making arrangements to contact them, and encouraging them to ring me if they wished. I phoned every day, and each time the wife was appreciative of contact but said 'We are doing a lot of sharing with a lot of tears and we need more time.' When I did go back several days later, I found the patient sitting up playing cards with his brother-in-law, and his wife feeling confident that she could now cope with his care. In fact, he died at home under the care of his GP and the district nurses, spending only his last twenty-four hours completely confined to bed, and regained quality in his life and relationships in the last six weeks that were left to him.

This may seem to be a dramatic example, but it also demonstrates that the nurse's presence can serve as a catalyst to relationships. In this particular case the mere presence of a third person was more influential than what was actually said in enabling this couple to break down for themselves the communication barriers caused by serious illness, in order to function as the close couple they usually were.

It goes without saying that at the time of death relatives need a lot of support. Even when death had been long expected, it always causes a great deal of shock, and as well as emotional support, relatives need guidance in making arrangements. They need time to sit quietly before going home, time to talk with the nurse about what has just happened, and time to cry. Giving relatives clear instructions as to when to return for the certificate and belongings should avoid any upsetting confusion later. If the family is present at the death they may want to remain at the bedside for a while afterwards. They may also request to see the body again after last offices have been performed, so attention to the patient's appearance is always necessary.

If the family were not present at the time of death they may want to see the body when they attend the hospital after the death. This is a sensitive issue for the nurse, who should not deny the family this important last gesture, whilst not forcing it upon those who really do not want it. Many relatives do not necessarily ask to see the dead person, but if they do so this can help them to come to terms with the reality of the death. Therefore the opportunity to see the body has to be offered in such a way that the relatives feel free to refuse.

The nurse accompanying the family should remember that this may be their first experience of death, and, for example, warn them not to be surprised if they find that the patient's skin may be cold to touch. The nurse should allow relatives to express their grief as they wish, and she may feel it is right to leave them alone for a while. It is as well to remember that some cultures express grief very differently from ours, and the result may be a dramatic display of strong emotions. Afterwards, the relatives may need to be gently helped to leave the body.

Enabling the relatives to see their dead relation in this way may be the first step in helping them to grieve. I recall a number of relatives who regretted not doing so, and making remarks like 'I often wonder if it was really him in the coffin and if he really has gone.' If hospital facilities do not cater well for those important experiences, relatives may be referred to the undertaker.

Conclusion

This chapter has looked at ways in which the nurse can communicate with the dying and their relatives. It is impossible in one chapter to cover all the problems and stresses that death brings, and the complexity of nursing the terminally ill. It is important that nurses should continue to learn something from every new situation and every new patient. It is also important to guard against imposing our own standards upon those we care for, as all people need to feel that they continue to have some control over their own lives even if they are suffering great physical disability. For this reason it is necessary to know when to stand back and not to intrude. Some patients respond to firm management, whereas others need to question and be part of the decision-making process. It is essential to try to understand patients' feelings and allow them to keep their freedom as individuals. This may mean accepting that our efforts in communication will not always appear to be helpful. For example, there will always be patients and relatives who cannot share and talk as we would like them to, just as there will be some patients who remain in despair and others who, in spite of instructions and explanation, choose not to take their pain-killing drugs regularly.

Perhaps more than any other member of the caring team, the nurse is in a strong position to gain the patient's confidence and establish a relationship with both him and his family. In writing this chapter I have assumed that nurses are allowed the freedom to communicate openly and honestly with dying patients. Of course, this is not so in every hospital. Situations still remain where only the doctor or the ward sister are allowed to deal with patients' searching questions, although in some circumstances they may well be the right people to do so, as the nurse may not feel able to give the information asked for.

Once nurses are given this freedom to communicate with the dying, they will need the full support of senior team members and will require the opportunity to discuss problems. This will also serve an educational purpose, for all dying patients have a lot to teach us, both personally and professionally, and confidence can only be gained by practical experience, and careful thought. Lastly, it is important to emphasise that the nursing care should not end with the patient's death. Having supported the family thus far we should be aware of their continuing needs in bereavement. However, bereavement after-care may not come into the regular sphere of duty for every nurse, although those working in terminal care units or in the community may well find themselves involved in this work.

This chapter has conveyed some of the demands made on those who nurse the terminally ill and support their relatives. It *is* both physically and mentally demanding work, and it requires the highest nursing skills combined with great sensitivity. Death is something everyone needs help with facing, and the time to prepare for it cannot be repeated.

References

Bluebond-Langner M. (1978) *The Private Worlds of Dying Children.* Princeton University Press

Bond S. (1978) *Processes of Communication about Cancer in a Radiotherapy Department.* Unpublished PhD Thesis: University of Edinburgh

Cartwright A. Hockey L. & Anderson J. (1973) *Life before Death.* London: Routledge & Kegan Paul

Glaser B. G. & Strauss A. L. (1965) *Awareness of Dying.* London: Wiedenfield Nicholson

Kubler-Ross E. (1973) *On Death and Dying.* London: Tavistock Publications

McIntosh J. (1977) *Communication and Awareness in a Cancer Ward.* London: Croom Helm

OPCS (1979) *Mortality Statistics 1977: England & Wales.* Series DHI No. 5. London: HMSO

Parkes C. M. (1972) *Bereavement – Studies of Grief in Adult Life.* London: Tavistock Publications

Raven R. W. (ed) (1975) *The Dying Patient.* London: Pitman Medical

Saunders C. M. (1976) *Care of the Dying.* London: Macmillan

Saunders C. M. (ed) (1978) *The Management of Terminal Disease.* London: Arnold

Chapter 10

Postscript

Jill Macleod Clark   Will Bridge

In this, the final chapter, we have the difficult task of bringing together all the issues, insights, problems, and possible solutions which the preceding chapters have covered under the general heading of 'communication in nursing'.

We started the book by observing that the term 'communication' is a vague and over-used word in many walks of life, not least in nursing. However, by now, the importance and pervasiveness of the activities which go to make up communication in nursing should be clear. In Chapter 1 we suggested that this variety of activities could be thought of as a range or a continuum, extending from, say, giving or collecting factual information to establishing close, supportive, and sometimes emotional relationships with patients. The eight preceding chapters have each tackled and explored some aspects of this range of activities which are relevant to the needs of particular groups of patients.

The contributions in retrospect

The first chapter, contributed by Jenifer Wilson Barnett, concentrated largely upon the exchange of information between nurses and patients admitted to general medical or surgical wards. In doing so she cited a convincing number of studies which clearly show that patients both want and gain measurable benefits from information and explanation about what to expect on admission to hospital, about operations, investigations, or their discharge back into the community. Thus, even in a field of patient care which is increasingly characterised by short stays, intensive medical treatment and early discharge, communication has a vital part to play in nursing care.

Various chapters have shown that different areas of nursing pose different kinds and levels of communication difficulties. For certain types of patients, such as those in intensive care units, the confused elderly, or the psychiatrically disturbed, the nurse encounters fundamental barriers to communication. For example, at different times the nurse must deal with patients who cannot hear, patients who will not hear, patients who cannot see, and patients who will not respond to the nurse. Such circumstances have served to focus the contributors' attention upon the most detailed elements of communication in, for example, psychiatry (Chapter 6), and the intensive care unit (Chapter 5). Thus, the psychiatric nursing chapter included an analysis of possible listening behaviours and responding skills, and in the chapter focusing upon intensive care, this analysis included an extensive list of the factors which can inhibit communication with critically ill patients. Different issues were raised when paediatric nursing or community nursing were considered. In these areas (and several others) communication involves the parents or relatives as much as the patient himself. This extra dimension of communication often presents special problems, when relatives have to be helped to play their part in caring for the patient whilst themselves feeling helped and supported.

We have seen that there are many situations in which nurses are involved in strategies or tactics and counter-tactics with patients and relatives. These are brought out quite clearly in the chapters on cancer nursing and nursing in the community. However, sophisticated communication tactics are also often required in paediatrics where the parents may need help to come to terms with and care for a sick child, and in geriatrics where many patients need to be encouraged to develop their independence and self-confidence.

Care of the dying seems to involve all the above issues, plus a few more. As a result of this, Maggie Hacking's chapter is the longest in the book. In caring for patients suffering from terminal illnesses, nurses face problems concerning how much and what information to give, how best to get this information across, how to help the patient and relatives to adjust, what tactics to employ in order to protect themselves, and how to deal with anxious friends and relatives. This final contributed chapter, in common with virtually all the preceding chapters, concluded that in order to rise to these challenges, nurses need specific training and preparation in communication skills, and support and counselling when they put these skills into practice.

The need for educational change

Although this book started by focusing firmly upon nurse-patient communication, the preceding chapters have raised a number of fundamental questions and issues about the nature of nursing itself. Many of the lessons to be learnt from this book have important implications for nurse education. An inspection of the various syllabuses in nurse education shows that a certain amount of lip service is now being paid to the need for training in nurse-patient communication. However, little of this lip service is being turned into practice. Considering the importance of communication in nursing, the amount of teaching time allocated to the topic in most educational programmes is disappointingly low.

There are a number of reasons for this situation, and some have been mentioned earlier in the book. First of all, teachers and experienced ward staff are inclined to view communication as a pleasant optional extra which does not directly contribute to the patients' well-being or rate of recovery. The contributed chapters have presented a good deal of evidence showing that this is not an accurate view. Similarly, it is widely imagined that the ability to communicate cannot be taught, or at least, cannot be learnt. Again, the preceding chapters and a growing body of research literature in the social sciences both show this to be incorrect.

Practical methods of teaching communication should be developed in nursing as they have been developed in other fields such as school teaching, general practice, and even commerce and industry. These professions are increasingly recognising the key role played by communication in their day-to-day work and have responded to this new priority in a number of ways; particularly by means of important developments in their programmes of initial training and continuing education. Thus, for example, techniques of videotaped feedback for teaching communication skills are widespread in institutions which train school teachers (McIntyre *et al.* 1976); and management training involves similar educational approaches as well as role play and other activities focusing on the topic of communication (Rackham & Morgan 1977).

Many of these training programmes have been evaluated, and the results indicate that they can have measurable, lasting and positive effects upon professional communication behaviour (see, for example, Ellis 1979; Kagan 1975). The data from such studies do not support the view often expressed in nursing that communication is a subject which cannot be taught. As a result, it is no longer appropriate to encourage the attitude that, as far as communication is concerned . . . 'You are either born with it, or you are not'. Changes in the content of training programmes in nursing will only succeed in establishing a higher priority for communication with patients if they are part of a broader picture of educational and organisational change. This will inevitably take time and it will have to be a gradual process. First of all, we need more knowledge both about the characteristics of effective and ineffective communication in nursing, and the teaching methods which will help to develop nurses' communication skills. This will require both nursing research initiatives and the utilisation of research findings from other fields where the problems of communication are also being tackled.

Secondly, the tutorial staff themselves need to be trained in these areas. This is no easy matter, since knowledge of the processes of communication will have to compete for space in curricula already heavily loaded with far more established subjects such as anatomy and physiology. Tutorial staff may also find that the methods required for teaching communication are novel and even uncomfortable, since experience in other professions indicates that teachers may have to use relatively unfamiliar techniques such as small-group teaching, audiotape and videotape feedback, role play, and so on (Argyle 1972). Thus, teachers of nursing will need a good deal of help in order to include the teaching of communication in their courses.

The next stage in any plan of campaign to improve nurse-patient communication must involve educating the trained clinical staff. The experience of contributors to this book, and of nursing researchers elsewhere, for example, Pembrey (1980), suggests that ward sisters and other trained clinical staff play a key role influencing the working atmosphere, and hence the priority given to communication on any given ward. Thus, training in communication skills and an understanding of the contribution they make to patient care must become part of the background of all experienced nurses in the future.

There can be little doubt that student nurses need education in the field of nurse-patient communication right from the start of their training. However, this seems unlikely to be effective until experienced ward staff have sufficient commitment to allow time and energy to be devoted to communicating with patients. Nor will it be effective if the subject of nursing communication is fitted into the teaching programme as an optional and untested extra. Student nurses should be given the opportunity to learn about the importance, diversity, and complexity of communication in patient care. They should also be given the resources to study their own patterns of communication by means of videotaped feedback and recordings. In addition, they need opportunities to practise communication skills in artificial situations using simulation and role play, as well as being encouraged to apply this learning in their day-to-day dealings with patients.

The educational developments and corresponding changes in nursing practice described above raise two further important issues – the first relates to nurses' feelings of involvement with patients and their consequent need for support, and the second concerns the different roles which nurses adopt, and the effects that these roles have upon communication with patients.

Involvement with patients

One particular objection to attempts to improve nurse-patient communication is quite often voiced. This is that closer communication may result in the nurse becoming too involved in the inevitable difficulties and sufferings of her patients. Indeed, in her analysis of hospitals as social systems, Menzies (1960) suggested that hospital systems, and the professions that work within them, are geared to promote non-communication with patients, in order to act as a defence mechanism against the anxiety which would result from excessive 'involvement'.

In response to this genuine concern, it is important to go back to the inadequacy of the term 'communication', and the large number of different levels and kinds of nursing activities which might be thought of as coming under the heading of 'nurse-patient communication.' At several points in this book we have described nursing communication as a continuum of skills ranging from the passing of factual information, through support and reassurance, to the sharing of feelings and emotions (this continuum was depicted in

Figure 1.1, page 3). We have also highlighted the wide range of tangible and intangible improvements in the patients' well-being and rate of recovery which result from improved communication at every point in this continuum. Therefore the nurse's commitment to patient care inevitably involves a commitment to close communication, and the problem becomes one of helping *her* to cope with this situation rather than expecting *the patient* to cope with non-communication. To put it another way, close communication with patients is not a risk taken by unprofessional or inexperienced nurses; it should be an essential aspect of the role of every nurse.

In practice, the kinds of communication required by most patients need not threaten their nurses to any significant degree. Nurse-patient communication at the factual and informational end of the 'communication continuum' described previously need not depend upon nor result in increased involvement. In fact, most nurse-patient conversations take place at this factual and informational level where we also have the most convincing research data about the physiological and psychological benefits of improved nurse-patient communication.

Some recent research (Faulkner 1979; Macleod Clark 1981) has been concerned with analysing aspects of these routine conversations between nurses and patients. Audio and videotape data have been gathered of nurses talking to patients on the wide range of routine and procedural matters which occupy a large proportion of the nurses' time. The analysis of these data shows that, even in non-threatening situations, nurses often speak to patients in ways which do not encourage communication. For example, nurses use verbal tactics like closed or leading questions ('You're feeling better today aren't you?') in order to control conversations, and their vocabulary inhibits anything other than superficial communication ('We're just going to give you a little prick in your botty'). Findings from research such as this do indicate that there may be many aspects of communication in nursing which could be improved without the risk of 'involvement' with patients.

This risk does exist, however, where nurse-patient communication concerns feelings and emotions, and particularly in situations which might best be described as 'counselling'. It seems likely that as different categories of patients have different needs for communication, there will be many patients who have almost no need for communication at these deepest emotional levels. However, the contributed chapters dealing with, for example, care of cancer patients and patients who are dying show that there are times when patients and relatives need the special abilities of a nurse who is able to counsel them and communicate with them at this level. While such abilities can be learned, we are not necessarily advocating that all nurses should be taught counselling skills. Indeed, these are not the skills most needed by nurses working in many fields, nor are they skills which can readily be taught to all kinds of nurses. At this stage therefore, it may be more important to concentrate upon developing nursing communication at the other end of the continuum described previously, by improving the routine communication of information, explanation and preparation.

Nevertheless, if nurses are to improve their communication with patients, they will need support. The need for mutual support within the nursing hierarchy, and the key role of the ward sister in this respect has already been referred to, but other forms of support are also needed. If important nursing information is to be obtained when patients are admitted, and if information about a given procedure, investigation, or even discharge from hospital is to be accurately communicated to patients, then the nurse will also need administrative support. This includes access to information, pre-prepared admission histories, and patients' records or nursing care plans in which explicit details are given about the patients' communication needs as well as their needs for medication or treatment.

Those nurses who choose to work with patients who do require intense communication or counselling are in special need of training and emotional support for themselves. In certain areas of patient care, anxiety and over-involvement are particularly likely, and the experienced staff on such wards should see it as their task to care for their nurses as well as their patients.

Roles and goals in nursing communication

The idea that nurses and patients adopt a range of roles in order to achieve their own goals has been developed in a number of chapters. Two such roles were described in Chapter 7, on community nursing, where Jean McIntosh drew from her own research data two possible roles – those of 'guest' in a household, and the professional 'nurse'.

The conversational examples in Chapter 7 clearly indicate that the role adopted by a nurse can profoundly effect her communication with patients. For example, the community nurse acting in the 'guest' role, perhaps with a patient who is compliant and coping well with his illness, would tend to use communication tactics conveying support, advice, and co-operation. This contrasts with the professional 'nurse' role which would communicate detachment and authority to, say, an unco-operative or overdependent patient However, using this perspective to improve communication in the community might not involve completely cutting out the professional 'nurse' role. Rather, by becoming more aware of their own behaviour, community nurses could be helped to evaluate and adapt their various roles, and limit their use of the 'professional nurse' to situations in which they would not otherwise be able to cope.

A little thought, or further investigation, would enable us to suggest other roles adopted by nurses working in other areas. For example, nurses working in hospital might find that they sometimes adopted the role of 'medical assistant', whereas at other times they were the 'patients' informer', 'health educator', or 'rehabilitator'. Again, each role implies a different style of nurse-patient communication, and the value of analysing roles is to alert nurses to the danger of restricting the range of roles which they play, such that they habitually adopt only one role irrespective of the patients' needs.

Theorising about human roles, and attempting to understand interpersonal behaviour using role analysis, has become widespread amongst social scientists, and some of their more broadly-based analyses may help in our understanding of nursing communication. One scheme which has already been applied to nursing is the role classification in Berne's *Transactional Analysis* (Berne 1974). This distinguishes between three possible roles in human communication; those of 'parent', 'adult', and 'child'. A brief description of these three roles (which Berne calls 'ego states') is given below:

Parent: When an individual is playing the role of a 'parent' in Berne's terminology, he is acting in the way he saw his own parent's act towards him when he was a child. The parent role is characterised by being assertive and autocratic, appearing to do things for the good of other people (particularly the 'child'), but taking little account of other people's opinions or expressions. In almost every respect, the 'parent' role involves talking down to people, and belittling them.

Child: A person playing the 'child' role is reverting to the habits, expressions, and ways of dealing with the world which he learnt and practised when he was a child. The role is characteristically passive, as the 'child' expects things to be done for him. He neither deals with the world through logic nor through autocratic pronouncements, but rather the 'child' tries to influence or cajole events. However the 'child' is unaffected by cynicism, and he is thoroughly dependent upon the support and love of others. 'Children tend to be spontaneous with their laughter, love and tears.

Adult: When a person is acting in the 'adult' ego state, he is acting rationally and logically, making decisions based solely upon information being received from the outside world. Old habits of parenthood, and childhood do not colour his judgements, attitudes or his ways of behaving. The 'adult' is autonomous rather than dependent, and, if we are to survive it is our 'adult' ego state which helps us with many day-to-day decisions such as when to cross a busy road, or what to put on the shopping list.

It is possible to recognise the relevance of this analysis to nursing communication. For example there is often a temptation for a nurse to act the 'parent' ('What are you doing up, you know you're supposed to be on bedrest?') and as a result the patient may respond in the role of a compliant or rebellious child ('Nobody ever tells me anything . . .'). Again, the value of carefully analysing what happens when nurses and patients communicate using schemes such as Berne's is that they will help the nurse to become more aware of how she relates to patients now, and what choices there are for the future. In this way she may be able to recognise and limit her use of any habitual and stereotyped nursing roles to situations in which they are desirable or where they are being used consciously and for a specific purpose.

Perspectives on nurse-patient communication

Like most books about nursing or any other field of health care, this book is written from the viewpoint of the professional nurse rather than from the perspective of the patient or client. This is manifest in the structure of the book, which treats nurse-patient communication in terms of a number of specialised areas of hospital and community care, and also in the list of contributors, which is made up of nurses rather than patients! Although we have already argued that these characteristics were necessary, given the state of the art in communication, it is important to explore the insights which would result from a more patient-centred perspective on nurse-patient communication.

To start with, patients are changing. Chapter 4 shows that they are getting older, and many of the other chapters show that they, and their relatives, may be becoming far less willing to accept a totally passive role in their diagnosis, treatment and care. The issue of accountability is also coming to the fore, and this is demonstrated by the fact that increasing numbers of patients and relatives make formal complaints as a result of mistakes, omissions, and inadequacies. It is likely that problems such as these will be far more widely recognised and discussed in health care in the future.

Changes in patients' needs will inevitably affect nursing communication. The growing geriatric population will result in increasing numbers of nurses involved with the elderly who will have to discover and develop the special communication skills. Equally, those caring for somewhat younger patients, who are increasingly articulate and questioning, will have to develop skills of teaching and consulting patients, and providing them with intelligent information about their care. As well as closer and more informative nurse-patient communication, this will require important changes in the ways which nursing care is planned, evaluated, and recorded (see Hunt & Marks-Maran 1980).

The key point about patients' own perceptions of nurse-patient communication is that they are likely to be at least as accurate and important as the nurses' perceptions. This may not always be the case in other aspects of health care, such as diagnosis and treatment, where patients' lack of specialised knowledge inevitably limits their ability to evaluate the care they receive. Nevertheless, nurses would clearly learn a great deal about the communication aspects of nursing care if they were to see it as a patient does.

Nurses and doctors are themselves patients and clients at various times, and it is significant that reports of their experiences usually concentrate upon the shortcomings and lessons they have learnt about *communication* during their time on the receiving end (see, for example, Viner 1975). Given that the patients' perspective is so vital in learning about communication, it may be worth considering how nurses could be put into the patients' shoes in as realistic a manner as possible, and helped to remember the patients' perspective throughout their professional lives.

Conclusion

In many respects this book only starts to scratch the surface of nursing communication. Indeed, in comparison with the weighty volumes about the medical and physical aspects of nursing, the small amount of literature on the topic of communication should be an embarrassment to the whole of the nursing profession.

So far, the research and investigations which we have been able to compile have largely been descriptions of the prevailing *status quo*. Even these descriptions leave large blank areas, such as communication in midwifery, in the accident and emergency department, in the out-patient clinic, and in family planning. However, in other fields of nursing, ample evidence has been cited for the fact that improved communication actually affects patients' physical well-being. Therefore a ward where talking to patients is frowned upon or given low priority is not just an unfriendly place in which to be ill; it is also a place in which the patient is likely to *suffer* a slower rate of recovery, greater pain, or increased anxiety. So far, such evidence relates largely to the communication of facts and information. It is important to extend out knowledge by looking at the effects of other aspects of nurse-patient communication, such as reassurance, touch and empathy.

Beyond this, if communication in nursing is to be improved, it will be important to undertake experimental research into this aspect of nursing. New tactics and strategies for encouraging communication on the ward need to be developed, and new teaching approaches such as the use of videotaped feedback will need to be pioneered and evaluated.

This book adopts many perspectives; draws from many disciplines; and leaves many loose ends. Readers who expected it to provide all the answers may be disappointed, but will be left with thought provoking ideas, and yet more new questions. Many of these questions are about the nature and purpose of nursing itself. This is because, as we pointed out earlier, when we asked the eight contributors to this book to write about communication in patient care, they ended up by describing problems and situations which are clearly at the heart of nursing in their own special areas of experience. No one can claim to be an expert on nurse-patient communication at this stage, but some nurses have obviously given it a great deal more thought than others. This book contains some suggestions for straightforward and immediate improvements in communication with patients, as well as suggestions for more fundamental and long-term changes. All these changes are essential if nursing is to continue developing as a profession which cares for patients as people.

References

Argyle M. (1972) *The Psychology of Interpersonal Behaviour.* Harmondsworth: Pelican Books

Berne E. (1974) *Games People Play.* London: Pitman

Ellis R. (1979) Simulated social skill training for the interpersonal professions. Paper presented at Annual NATO Conference *Analysis of Social Skills*, June 1979, Leuven

Faulkner A. (1979) Monitoring nurse-patient conversation on a ward. *Nursing Times,* 30 Aug., Occasional Paper

Hunt J. & Marks-Maran D. (1980) *Nursing Care Plans – The Nursing Process at Work.* Aylesbury: HM+M Publishers

Kagan N. (1975) Influencing human interaction – eleven years with IPR. *Canadian Counsellor,* 9(2), 74–97

McIntyre D., Macleod G. & Griffiths R. (1976) *Investigations of Microteaching.* London: Croom Helm

Macleod Clark J. (1981) Communication in nursing: analysing nurse-patient conversations. *Nursing Times,* 77(1), 12–18

Menzies J. (1960) A case study of the functioning of social systems as a defence against anxiety. *Human Relations,* 13(2), 95–123

Pembery S. E. M. (1980) *The Role of the Ward Sister in the Management of Nursing.* Unpublished PhD thesis, University of Edinburgh

Viner E. (1975) In Chaney P. (ed) Ordeal. *Nursing,* 5(6), 27–40